The Death of a Culture

Understanding the War: Animal Rights vs. Animal Welfare

—————

Second Edition

—————

David Fritsche Th. D.

The Death of a Culture

Copyright © 2010 by Dynamix Worx LLC
Publications

ISBN-13:978-1456403652

ISBN-10:1456403656

Dedication

To my wife Linda who loves the dogs as I do.

To my daughter Alycia who is my partner in the world of dogs and without whose help this book would not have been written.

Partners in my world of dogs!

A special thanks to Dana McKee for her editorial help with this second edition.

A special 'Thank You' to Gloria Birch for the cover picture. Gloria Birch and Cappy Pottle at Covy-Tucker Hills have been an inspiration to many as advisors and mentors in the world of German Shepherds.

Covy-Tucker Hill's Rachmaninoff
Greatly loved - Never forgotten

Table of Contents

Foreword

The Animal Culture Clash

It was a tense setting, as I stood before the crowd of police officers and administrators. It was late April 1992 and South Las Angeles was erupting into yet another race riot following the acquittal of four Los Angeles Police Officers who were tried for police brutality in the Rodney King incident. The Congress Woman from the Watts District was on TV justifying the eruption in terms I could not understand. I watched the television as she talked, saw her lips moving, heard the words she said, but could not understand the reasoning behind her justification. I recognized that her reality and perception of life was so different from my own that I had no frame of reference by which to understand what she was saying.

But that was earlier in the morning. Now, shortly after lunch, I was to address a convention of police officers, administrators and police chaplains. I had two hours to talk to them about "Cultural Awareness," and I could feel the tension. Most of the classes I had attended on the subject were pleas by some minority advocate calling for the class to understand the history of abuse of their culture and why they had a right to be angry. Here I was in the middle of a nationally televised race riot, teaching a cultural awareness class to police officers. Not an easy task - not easy at all.

I had developed some illustrations for the class, and so I put one on the projector and started in. As I went along I found what I thought was the appropriate time and stopped to talk about the current national crisis. Shots had been fired in various cities, fires were burning in communities up and down the West Coast and shots had been fired in Las Vegas. Our own community, Reno, Nevada, was on high alert and all days off were canceled for our local police agencies. We were prepared for war.

Following the class, I was humbled to see a spontaneous response of applause and then one officer jumped to his feet, followed by a ripple effect until the entire audience was standing and clapping. Then they came to talk, shake hands and tell me of their appreciation. I understood what was happening, although I did not expect this response. They were, for the first time, able to put the conflict into a context. Where they were expecting to be railed on and accused of being insensitive Neanderthals, I had instead given them a context in which to understand what was occurring - a clash of cultures - and why. One Chief of Police from the Southern part of our country said simply, "Reverend, I had never thought of our racial problems in the context you presented. This is the best class on the subject I have ever heard. Thank you for cutting across the B. S. and getting to the real issues."

We are in another war. It is not racial or ethnic but it is real, and it is serious. We are in a war against a way of life that embraces animals as a key part of normal life and a culture shift that wants to eliminate animals from being owned as personal property. Huge animal rights organizations have risen up proposing to save animals from abuse. They raise millions upon millions of dollars, little to none of which goes to help animals directly. They use names that sound humane, but they own no shelters, contribute to no local shelters and use the entire amount of money raised to pay lobbyists and to propose and support anti-breeding legislation. In 2009, 147 pieces of legislation were submitted in 37 states, all with similar provisions and wording.

6

Was there a central command post from which this effort was coordinated, or did all of these states just coincidentally happen upon the same words to solve the same perceived problem? How are we supposed to understand why a group of vegans have assumed command of our legislative process and demanded that companion animals be limited, eliminated and/or elevated in legal status from personal property to individuals having rights, animal rights? Thus animals have standing in court to sue their masters, owners or human companions. How is it that people from some recent cultural shift can interject their will into our relationship with our pets? They then presume to represent them against us - casting the pet-owning public in the role of brutish beasts that need to be controlled by strict legislation lest they ruin our world?

The following chapter is the essence of the class taught at the police convention. Possibly it will allow us to fathom contextually what is happening and help us find the path to peace in this war. Possibly animals will cease being victims of the warring camps, and we will be allowed a way of life that is historic, enjoyable and free from those radical extremists who want to save us from ourselves.

Introduction

Change is often described as a process that one third of the people watch happen, one third make happen and one third do not know it is happening. That may be true in our dog world. There is a war going on which will determine whether or not our animal agricultural interests and pet ownership will exist a few years from now. How that will be determined will be based on our response to the war and our ability to resist the Animal Rights agenda that has gained a legislative upper hand.

I invite you to come along for a few pages of orientation to the problem and then to enjoin the war. If you love your animals and want to continue to enjoy your relationship with them, then war is your only choice. Neither you nor I started it, but it is here none-the-less. The end of the story is yet to be determined. It will be determined by our response...

Join me!

The Author

Chapter One

Culture Shift: Why Things Go Wrong

Sociologists have decided that markings on walls in caves, left by primitive cultures, were significant records of the life of the nomadic hunter-gatherer before history books were written. None of them agree with me that it was probably teenage graffiti made by marauding gangs. OK, I agree; I am just being cynical about how we interpret what happened in prehistory. Given the myriad historical perspectives of reality, it is hard to be serious about 'scientific certainties.'

The Hunting-Gathering Culture

We do know something about our predecessors. They were largely nomadic, because they did not yet understand the finer points of agriculture. They gathered their food, and when the supply was depleted, they moved on in search of more. One hundred percent of their time and energy was expended in the search for food. Whatever they found was theirs. If they were skilled enough to kill an animal, the hunters were celebrated as heroes, and the family and tribe was fed. If not, they starved. Life was simple, and its simplicity was determined not by their lack of alternatives but by the worldview they held. Their laws, rules and traditions were shaped by that worldview, and their religions were also a reflection of their sense of reality.

If the hunt or the gathering went well, then the gods were happy with them; but if not, then certainly the gods were angry.

Authority enforced rules. Rules governed the discovery and distribution of food. While it may seem simple by today's cultural standards, humankind has always had the ability to create a rather elaborate social structure about its realities. So, through our discovery of ancient markings and implements, we have a view into the hunting-gathering cultures of the past. And yet it is not just from cave markings from the cave man era, but also from realities of that culture that remain in parts of our world, even until today.

The handiest picture is here in our own United States of America since the 'discovery' of the New World by Columbus. Of course the continent was here before Columbus came and did not need 'discovering' from the perspective of the natives who inhabited the land. They knew they were here and did not need documentation of that fact from a European explorer. But the advent of Columbus' arrival on these shores brought an eventual influx of settlers and a massive cultural conflict. Somewhere in Europe, many, many years before, the hunting-gathering culture had given way to another worldview. Someone, we do not know who, stood and thought about the plants being harvested in their hunting-gathering culture, and that person surmised that roots, berries, nuts were there because they grew by some mysterious process. They also discovered that by intervening in that process, one could control it, and they would not have to travel all the time looking for food but could stay in one location and grow food.

The Agrarian Culture

The revelation of the agricultural operation created an entirely new procedure and an entirely new cultural context. Now the tribe did not have to move from place to place looking for food but could cultivate and harvest what they grew by agricultural work where they were. The shift in worldview and in human activities and ways of thinking was enormous. The shift in conclusion is obvious. If I plant a crop, water it and harvest it, it is now no longer available to the nomadic traveler to gather. In the hunting-gathering culture, if one finds a crop, he is a hero, but in the agricultural setting if they find and take my crop, they are a thief. Private property is an invention of the agricultural world view. Before that, the hunter-gatherer viewed the whole world as open to anyone and viewed themselves as part of the earth and the great spirits. Farming culture, agriculture changed all of that.

So Columbus did not come and confiscate the land of the native Indians of America. The natives did not view it as their land, that is, as private property. The land did not belong to them; they belonged to the land. The crops that the settlers planted and the animals they raised were not theirs to own but were available to be found, hunted and harvested. Neither side of the culture clash had any way of understanding or communicating their different mindset and worldview to the other.

The Industrial Culture

But the plot thickens as we move along in history. Somewhere, in some part of some continent, lived an ingenious person who thought for a minute or two and decided that if his property grew great hay but not great horses, that he could trade his hay for the horses that his friend bred on the other side of the valley. Thus by the specialty of effort, both would prosper. As this specializing of effort and productivity took hold, we entered the industrial age. The agricultural age of farms and ranches

11

gave way to greater specialty, and factories sprang up to process food, distribute it, and do it quickly. Humans had time now to do something other than just find food. The end result was a population shift from the country to the city and proximity to the factory. Now, rather than the dominant, self-sufficient family farmer, the farm changed to become the corporate enterprise. And the family, rather than growing its own food, earned money to buy it by working for someone else. A whole new way of looking at the world again altered the laws, the sense of cultural structures, and the activities of people.

With the increase of productivity and specialization came also a new phenomenon on the planet, leisure time. Humanity was not required to give one hundred percent of their time to finding food; they had time after their eight-hour shift to play, socialize, and be entertained. The shape of their world changed to include things that were never imagined in the beginning of human civilization. Entertainment and sporting activities now interjected themselves into the world, and competed for time and money.

Culture	Hunter/Gatherer	Agricultural	Industrial	Information	AR Culture
Land	Belong to the earth	Ownership of property	Utilitarian ownership	Real property insignificant	Back to: Belonging to the land
Religion	Plural gods of nature	Mono-theistic personal God	Church as corporate enterprise	Personal & Private	Reversion to Pantheism
Law	Tribal/ situational	Regional/ codified	Codified/ Rule of law	Over-codified/Loss of discretion	Loss of personal property
Power	Might makes right	Ability to produce/ Personal power	Police power (delegated)	Use of information	Political correctness
Family	The tribe	Nuclear	Schedule driven nuclear	Undefined	Alternative
Rights	Tribal. survival	Individual/ family	Individual/ minority	Nationalized	Generalized/ ill-defined
Wealth	Strength, gathering skills	Productivity of family	Tangible assets	Control of information	Control of philosophy

And so goes the formation of culture around worldview. As comprehension changes (or presumption, as the case may be) so do the forms and structures of culture. It affects not just how we get our mega-needs filled (food, shelter, human relationships) but our meta-needs as well (meaning, personal value, worth, etc.) The rules of a culture can change so drastically transitioning to the next, that the hero becomes the criminal, and the owner becomes the abuser. It is not that the activity of the individual changes but the context that judges the act.

- Hunter-gatherer Culture: Find a cow, feed the tribe = Hero.
- Agrarian Culture: Find a cow in a yard, feed the tribe = Thief.
- Industrial Culture= Find a cow, check zoning and buy cow for processing.
- Information Culture= Find a cow, lookup cow on internet, determine statistical data about cows.
- AR Culture: Find the cow in a yard (Animal Rights view) = Owner is abusing by confining

How a culture processes information and judges action is not determined by some objective and eternal data but by the cultural assumptions it embraces. That is the essence of a cultural existence. It is the definition given to the relationships within a people group born out of a worldview. When the worldview changes, so do all of the rules and structures within the culture.

Families and Cultures

Nowhere is that better seen than in the structures of the family. In the hunter-gatherer culture, the basic unit of relationship is the tribe. Everything is designed for the survival of the tribe. The tribe is basically an extended family that grows by reproduction and stays together for mutual support in the process of survival. In that tribal structure, the elders rule by assignment of presumed wisdom, and the children are tended to in group. Although the children have biological parents, as a practical matter, the nomadic lifestyle predisposes the authority structures to be shared with other family members. The care and safety of the children as well as the rite of passage into adulthood is largely a tribal matter.

In the agrarian culture, families separate from the tribe, and though they may group together in communities, the farm setting predisposes them to a nuclear family with clear gender roles and work assignments. Dad and the sons go into the field to plow, plant and harvest, while the mother and daughters cook, clean, prepare and store what the guys produce.

But the family of the industrial culture takes a whole other shape. The modular family moves into the city, dad takes a job in the factory working from 8 – 5, and the children go off to school in the city school system. The family is fractured by schedules that do not mesh with each other; members are lucky to meet periodically in the evening and on weekends in the industrial age home.

As time goes on, the family in this culture changes in other ways. It is soon discovered that little Johnny is no longer an asset, no longer pulling his share of productive work on the family farm. He is now a liability, loved as he may be. He does not produce but consumes. The child of the agrarian culture increased the family's asset value by increasing productivity. But in the industrial culture, kids cost the family a fortune in schooling, clothing and education amounting to an estimated $300,000 per child. Children were great, but as their asset value became a liability, the size of the family changed in just a few short years from 8 or 9 children to 1.3 per household.

An easy way to see this shift still in process is to look at various subcultures in our world today and see their family size. Those who have fewer children tend to be better educated, more affluent/wealthy. In some ethnic minorities, their minority status is being threatened by the proliferation of reproduction. They won't remain a minority for long. And yet, within the current cultural norms, education and economic levels have not risen, leaving those subcultures at risk of failing to enjoy the fruit of past culture shifts.

The family of tomorrow may be something totally different, or to a large degree non-existent. The individualism of the latter part of the industrial culture and the beginning of the information culture may foreshadow the demise of the nuclear family. As alternative life styles and a general move away from our historic Judeo-Christian values and religious underpinnings sweep us into the next cultural norms, the family as we know it may disappear. Or it may be suspected of some evil intent as the hero hunter becomes the thief, so to speak.

As the Industrial Age gives way to the Information Age, everything changes again. This time, the whole basis of wealth moves from tangible assets to intellectual assets. The industrial corporation was wealthy because it had land, buildings and inventory, but the corporation of the information age grows wealthy because it controls information and distributes it at a profit. Our whole system of bookkeeping and our view of wealth is altered as bright young entrepreneurs rise from poverty and obscurity to amass wealth simply because of their programming skills.

Our legal system changes also with this shift in cultural context and cultural expectation. Bank robbery as the crime of greatest profit in the past now becomes practically impossible in the age of electronic surveillance and electronic transfer of assigned wealth, and cyber crime becomes the new target for the less than honest.

The family is also affected. Where Johnny used to come home from school and play baseball with his friends in the field down the street, now he isolates himself at his computer, Wii, or other individualized device, where he entertains himself for endless hours.

With each shift of culture arises a resulting conflict. Wars used to be fought by one nation against another, but today our wars are cultural. (Well, they have always been cultural, but in past generations the nationalism of a country embraced a cultural norm.) When there was a war it was because of the differences that one nation held toward the other, perceived or real, and those differences in reality focused that sense of threat into conflict. Today, nation states are not the cultural custodian they were in the past, as information and communications become global. Today we embrace multiculturalism as a way of allowing for individuality, but the result is, we have no culture. America's history is freely revised to fit each cultural worldview and each philosophical difference, so what used to be the melting pot of America is not melting. It is fermenting as the political correctness of a multicultural sensitivity defines no norm and permits the differences in reality that, in and of themselves, produce conflict.

We are a gracious and tolerant nation, but we are not good at producing a central focus and identity around which the entire nation can rally. Our greatest strength may well have become our greatest weakness. While we are arguing about our religious, political and ethnic differences, other parts of the world, who have a more focused national identity, are replacing us as the economic and industrial leaders in the world. The problem with our economic slide and our loss of respect in the world has little to do with the arrogance of the ugly American and far more to do with an inability to provide a central cultural identity around which we can gather. We are not only a nation of multi-ethnic groups; we are a nation which embraces multiple pockets of subcultures who share nothing in common. We have a broad range of gathering cultures still operating in our cities as gangs or cultural groups who have no contact with the agricultural world of the past, the industrial world of just a few years ago, and are totally unprepared to compete in the information age of the present.

Multiculturalism sounds nice and seems tolerant, but rather than creating a rich mosaic of a cultural jigsaw puzzle, it has left us with an incoherent and uncoordinated pile of subcultures who do not communicate, do not interface, and cannot be plugged into any sense of a combined reality.

In the meantime, the cultural tentacles of other subcultures have penetrated our boarders, leaving us unprepared to acknowledge that we are in a philosophical vacuum. We are left with no way to identify a religious extreme or a political extreme or a moral extreme as an enemy bent on our destruction. Culture shift, unless it happens to an entire nation, will leave that nation at odds with itself, operating in various realities, each of which cannot be understood by others.

Remember: As cultures shift, so do all of the rules and expectations. The nomadic gathering culture cannot understand the rules of the agricultural invention of private property, the right to the fruit of the harvest and the domestication of animals for food and work. The agricultural world cannot exist in the age of industrialization; it will be swallowed up by specialization and efficiency in greater supply at less cost. It cannot compete. So also, the industrial factory cannot continue to make buggy whips when the information age gives us computer-operated transportation and entertainment, and a wealth-shift from the tangible to the informational.

Chapter Two

A New Culture and a Rising Conflict: Why our culture is dying!

America was born in a seed plot of conflict. The despotic values of a British Empire had become a burden too great for the settlers in this new nation to endure. As a result the foundational words of our Declaration of Independence rang out:

> When in the Course of human events it becomes necessary for one people to dissolve the political bands which have connected them with another and to assume among the powers of the earth, the separate and equal station to which the Laws of Nature and of Nature's God entitle them, a decent respect to the opinions of mankind requires that they should declare the causes which impel them to the separation.
>
> We hold these truths to be self-evident, that all men are created equal, that they are endowed by their Creator with certain unalienable Rights, that among these are Life, Liberty and the pursuit of Happiness. — That to secure these rights, Governments are instituted among Men, deriving their just powers from the consent of the governed, — That whenever any Form of Government becomes destructive of these ends, it is the Right of the People to alter or to abolish it, and to institute new Government, laying its foundation on such principles and organizing its powers in such form, as to them shall seem most likely to effect their Safety and Happiness. Prudence, indeed, will dictate that Governments long established should not be changed for light and transient causes; and accordingly all experience hath shewn that mankind are more disposed to suffer, while evils are

sufferable than to right themselves by abolishing the forms to which they are accustomed. But when a long train of abuses and usurpations, pursuing invariably the same Object evinces a design to reduce them under absolute Despotism, it is their right, it is their duty, to throw off such Government, and to provide new Guards for their future security.

With the stroke of the pen, and many years of blood, sweat and tears, this nation became a new culture, defined by freedom from governmental excesses and hallmarked by guarantees that individual rights, which were given by God Himself, could not be infringed upon. But the nature of government being what it is, sooner or later it tries to solve more problems, provide more services, and in the course of that expansion of influence, grows larger, and more intrusive at the expense of individual responsibilities and freedoms.

Again, the family is a great place to see the effects of this swing of power. The doctrine of Parens Patria, or the "state as the parent" was primarily absent from our culture until about 60 years ago. In legal doctrine it existed, but in practice did not reach into the home to any extent. The state operated orphanages and adoption systems, but it was assumed that the family was responsible for themselves. The raising of children was assumed to be a parental right and responsibility. In the culture of the hunter-gatherer that was never an issue as the tribe took care of the children corporately with no higher authority to intervene. As the culture shifted and the nuclear family moved onto the farm, there was still no governmental issue, for the self-sustaining family had no need to be governed, and government had no precipitating issue with that cultural reality - the family.

But as the family changed in the industrial revolution and moved into the city, and mom and dad went off to work, things

20

changed. Johnny was no longer with dad all day in the field but was left after school to tend to himself until mom came home. The relationship of child to parent in the agricultural setting was one of constant presence with one another; in the industrial culture Johnny spends most of his time with his peers and teachers and less time with his parents. The nature of the family is drastically altered in this cultural shift. The greatest influences in Johnny's life become peer pressure and TV, neither of which reflects the sense of values and responsibility of the agricultural family.

These changes plus the growing divorce rate in this new culture become the setting where the state is now forced to pick up responsibility dropped by the troubled leaders of the nuclear family. A new phenomenon occurs in our land as police departments began to commission juvenile officers; our jail system expands to include juvenile halls. Little by little, government takes more and more responsibility not only to fix the broken family system and the fallout from it, but to assume the responsibility vacated by wayward parents. It is only a short step from that assumption of authority by the state to its directing the family as to how to parent, i.e., set rules about what constitutes proper parenting and what is abuse. This assumption of responsibility did not exist in the agrarian culture.

Step by step, well-meaning people, who sit in those seats of power and authority, presume that they should take responsibility. After all, they are hired to do a job, and certainly doing a responsible job is expected. So they inspect stuff, define terms, create expectations, issue normative directives. Before long the state is in charge of determining what a family looks like and how children are to be educated, raised, fed and nurtured. When the culture shifted from the farm to the city, a

21

shift in expectations of responsibility and the Controller of the definition of responsibility was also reassigned. The cultural expectations shifted from the assumption of expertise on the part of the parent to the assumption of greater expertise on the part of the social expert and the legal system.

As we move through our cultural progress, or process (we are not sure it is progress at all!) something else shifts. The rural world of the previous century also had a sense of social distance and tolerance, given that expertise was disseminated to the family and the local community. We presumed that the way we did things and the values we placed on the personal property we owned was our business and ours alone. We also assumed that how the neighbor, five miles down the road did things was their business. But as we enter our contemporary culture we are shocked to find that expertise is not ours but is resident in the experts; they have the power to determine what is the right way to do things and how life should be lived. So we have community standards administered by home owners associations, social organizations and expanded governmental bureaus who decide things for us that we previously decided on our own. We are told what color we can paint our house, what we can have in view in our yard and how many animals we can have on our property. We have become a culture of imposed expertise in which an elite opinion is honored as having value for everyone in the community, and less and less personal responsibility is permitted.

From the rule of the majority in larger national issues, to the rule of the minority in smaller community issues, our entire former structures and norms are sliding away from personal responsibility and personal power to pockets of expert control by governmental dictate. You do not have to be elected to office to rule over others. One has only to claim greater knowledge and expertise and get the government to verify that expertise.

So we live in an entirely different world than our fathers did. Insurance companies do not have to sell the value of insurance, for it is dictated by the government – citizens must have it. You do not have to deal with handling the trash you produce in your household; the government has decided and franchised a company to take care of it. You can agree to the system or they will bill you anyway – it is dictated. And we could go on illustrating the changes that have taken place in moving personal responsibility to a corporate, governmental base. Not all of those changes are evil, but whether they are excessive and evil or not, they are the result of a culture shift and of a restructuring of how we live together on this planet.

The problem is, not everyone has moved into this expected norm of governmental and expert oversight. There is conflict in our land, and it is being played out in a general sense of rebellion against the shift away from personal responsibility. Somewhere, deep in the roots of our national heritage, the expectation endures that we should carry our own weight, make our own decisions, take care of our own families and live our lives without the micromanaged controls of government detailing our use of personal property and liberties. The culture shift has gone way too far. Some predict that a national confluence of resistance to greater interference in our homes and lives is coming.

Nowhere is this conflict better seen than in the world of animals. Animals have been the constant companion to humans since time began. Animals have always provided or assisted the human family with work, food and clothing. But our cultural shifts have influenced our use of and relationship to animals. The family farm depended on animals for everything from pulling the plow, to guarding the flock, to becoming dinner for the family. In this sense, the agricultural culture shared its values with the hunter-gatherer culture. Animals were central to existence. But as we moved away from the farm and the necessity of that part of our dependence on animals, we also found the role of the animal redefined by the nature of city dwellers, the expectation of close neighbors and the changing shadow of government and experts who lobby for control.

The extent of that change is seen in the rise of the modern Animal Rights movement. This movement has grown from a few counter-culture weirdoes who wanted to save the bugs from car windshields to a modern enterprise of presumed expertise with multiple million dollar budgets. Those budgets are expended almost entirely on paid lobbyists proposing to know what is best for all animals and for us who relate to them. While government seems to be willing and able to accept their credentials, the animal world around them is not ready at all. Agricultural interests, animal exhibitors, breeders, hobbyists and even zoos are caught in the ever-increasing imposition of values that are uncomfortable at best and untenable at their extreme.

These organizations who propose animal rights are not suggesting that we need to be better at our ownership and care, but that animals' legal position in the world should be elevated to the same status as humans; that they can have standing in any suit in a court of law. They intend to change all legislative language from what has been traditional, the owners of animals, to the guardians of animals. They thus reduce the rights and responsibilities of the human companion and shift that power to the state or to the experts, which of course they purport to be.

This shift in definition and in the arena of power over animals is the issue in a conflict that is a war, not simply a discussion.

Animal Rights purists, of course, insist that animals should not be consumed for food. Their general goal is to create forced veganism on the general populous. By definition, a vegan is one who does not consume meat or other animal proteins - eggs, milk, cheese, etc. Former generations, coming out of the agricultural world, were willing to give place to the vegetarian who, because of religion or preference, did not eat meat. But we are less inclined to be told by the current generation of aggressive 'experts' how to live our lives and how to deal with our personal property - our animals.

In the last legislative session (2009), 147 pieces of animal legislation were proposed in 37 states, all with similar wording and issues. Many were related to how agricultural animals are housed and slaughtered. Most had to do with hobby breeders who breed dogs and cats for the domestic pet owner, and for their hobby, animal shows. Spay and neuter laws led the way with bans so stringent as to put a stop to all animal breeding, which aims to render America a 'petless' society within one animal generation. This has sparked a war of words, legislative testimony and the formation of voter blocks.

How this all plays out in the halls of legislatures in the future and in the culture in general has to do with more than just the companion animal and TV dog shows. It has to do with the extent of government and the acceptance of experts who are not involved in agriculture or animal sports, but propose to speak for the animals. Their effort to change the status of animals legally is in keeping with their desire to represent the animals in the courts against their owners. This is the conflict point, with a growing backlash from animal lovers in all segments of our society.

Animal Rights (AR) activities involve more than legislative lobbying. Activists are involved in animal terrorism. Their violence motivates the FBI to maintain a list of animal terrorist organizations and people who have acted out terrorist activities. Though AR demonstrations presume to be for the animals' good, they are carried out at the cost of the animals' safety. Several incidents of show dogs being released from their crates at dog shows is one way animal rights activist make their statement. They propose that animals be returned to the wild and not be confined by humans. The problem is, Mother Nature is not a kind and gentle, nurturing caretaker; rather, she is a ruthless and cruel serial killer. Weather, disease and predators are not kind to domesticated animals. Reaction from animal lovers of every kind is gathering momentum. As ignorant, meddlesome people take from us the right to be responsible and to control our own lives and property, it is war, pure and simple.

Chapter Three

The Catch 22 for Pure Bred Dogs

Many of the provisions of recent legislation either proposed (or proposed and passed) by states, counties and cities across the nation have similar provisions. Many were written at the request of these governmental subdivisions by the Humane Society of the United States, assuming that this agency somehow speaks for the United States, or is the agency overshadowing all humane societies or agencies in our communities. Nothing could be further from the truth. HSUS has no shelters and contributed less than 4% of its 120 million dollar annual budget to hands on shelter activities.

Yet, it is assumed to be the premier national agency speaking for the animals. What it really does is propose legislation that is not pro animal at all. There are several provisions of these proposed ordinances that are contradictory which are either proposed in abject ignorance or are possibly designed to lead to the frustration and demise of the animal culture and its reproductive abilities. Some of those conflicts are described as follows:

1. Exemptions for animal registries who have approved breeding standards.

General spay and neuter ordinances, usually have some exemptions which sound like they accommodate the breeding of animals, but which are part of the Catch 22 problem. For those of you who are too young to remember the book or movie titled

"Catch 22," it is about military orders and sanity during WWII. In the book, the main character could not fly combat missions unless he was deemed sane. But to fly them, he had to know the risk he was taking to his own safety and to the safety of the flight crew, which made him insane. So he could not fly the mission, but had to = Catch 22.

This same predicament is clearly written into much of the legislation proposed today, and many feel it is not through ignorance. It sort of sounds nice to exempt dogs from spay and neuter ordinances who are pure bred and registered by one of the many dog registries in our nation. Certainly the registry will provide the standards for breeding and assure that the animals produced meet "approved breeding standards." Although all breed clubs have a breed standard which describes the end result that all should be breeding for, none have breeding standards. Breeding is not manufacturing. Neither puppies nor kittens come down an assembly line where approved breed inspectors use micrometers and other measuring instruments to determine if they are assembled properly.

While animal genetics is making tremendous strides in discovering the animal genome and how genetics works, it is still in its infancy. Breeders do not have assembly line, standardized parts that get placed in the mechanism in a prescribed manner to end up as a perfect, guaranteed product at the end of the line. These are not mechanisms at all; they are organisms. Until we understand that simple distinction, we are doomed in terms of legislating the product. Organisms are the end result of a biological process in which genetic puzzles are assembled without our knowledge or permission into an end result, each of which is imperfect, yet wonderful.

So, for any breed club to attempt to dictate breeding practices is to assume understanding of how the gene gods work, and willingness to approve each breeding - and its result - while restricting others. The fact is, breeding involves the study of the history of other breedings and the results. Where problems are found, the program is adjusted away from the problem so that the genes cannot give the surprises they often do. It takes a lot of study, meticulous research, and in the end, it is at best an educated guess as to what the biological organisms will be. Most often, it is a delightful enterprise of the joyful participation in the resulting litter. Too often, it is a heartbreaking time of humbling in which we understand how little we know.

Thus, no breed club is going to standardize their breeding practices. They will hold to the standard and keep that banner waving as the goal, but there is no way for any breed club or registry to place their stamp of approval on one breeding program over others who are disapproved. To do so would be corporate suicide with their breeders on the one hand and an unrealistic legal liability for continuous suits by the breeders and the public on the other. That alone would be a Catch 22.

So, legislation which provides an exemption for registries with approved breeding standards is not an exemption at all. The City of Los Angeles recently passed sweeping spay and neuter laws that got rid of all the previous well meaning but contradictory exemptions. They were criticized for taking a direct slap at pure bred dogs, but in reality, they were only eliminating Catch 22 exemptions that could not be used anyway.

What most breed clubs do is hold the standard of the breed as the goal without approving any program or practice as to how to reach that standard. A majority of breed clubs follow a breeders' code of ethics that has to do with the expectation of

29

honesty and integrity with one another and the public, and has to do with the safety and sanitation of a breeding program. They also usually discourage the use of animals with known faults, either faults of the standard or faults of health in breeding programs. Of course, breed clubs cannot guarantee that those ethical standards are followed simply because of proximity to the property of each member and the understanding of personal property rights.

But all in all, the end result is a general improvement of each breed as time goes on, with an acknowledgment that occasionally there is a setback for a given litter, a given breeding line or even a breed wide trap that genetics produced and fallible humans did not see coming. Because of those surprises, some have advanced the theory that mixed breed dogs are superior genetically and in health. This would be impossible to establish in that mixed breed dogs do not have breeders who keep records, plan the breedings away from problems in the line, do not breed for any specific trait and do not usually take responsibility for the puppies or their breeding reputation after the litter is whelped and sold or given away. Mixed breed do have problems, but since they do not propose perfection and are not measured by a standard, they tend to fall under the radar, so to speak, of criticism for passing on genetic defects.

2. Exemptions for Show Dogs.

Most of the mandatory spay and neuter legislation provides an exemption for show dogs, realizing that most registries do not allow an altered dog to show. So an exemption is provided for show dogs, usually mandating that the exempt dog provide evidence of its show career by having been shown in a dog show approved by a recognized dog registry. Otherwise it must be spayed or neutered by three months of age, and there is the problem.

Most registries start the dog show classes at 6 months of age, so a dog cannot be a show dog until it is six months old or must be spayed or neutered by 3 months of age. Double bind? You bet. Add to that problem the fact that many show exhibitors do not show their dogs until they are old enough and mature enough to win. Each dog has a time when it is 'ready.' The exhibitor will know when that time is and, depending on the breed, it may be when the dog is two to three years old.

Some exhibitors, mostly newer members of the hobby will show every week somewhere hoping for a chance to win. But the more experienced will wait until their dog is ready and then will select the judges that might be partial to their style of dog. This way they can finish a dog (obtain his championship) in a shorter period of time and at less expense. Dog shows can be expensive, with the cost of travel, entries, handling fees and so forth mounting up to hundreds of dollars for a single weekend. So exhibitors have learned to be expeditious in their planning and to find the avenue of enjoying their hobby with the least cost.

All of that violates the age specific requirements of the current wave of legislation and places almost every show dog in a position where it could be fined, confiscated, and altered without the permission of the owner. The show enthusiast is placed in a position of either complying and not showing, or showing and violating the law. The exemption is meaningless and creates a no win situation for people.

Further, the laws are so generalized that they do not specify what constitutes a 'show dog.' The wording and aim seems to be toward the conformation show but that does not account for those dogs who do obedience, agility, rally, herding, tracking, field trials, schutzhund, or other sports in a long line of competitions that people do with their dogs. Or possibly the assumption is that one sport can reproduce to meet the demands of the ongoing involvement of the exhibitor, but the rest may not. Legislation, regardless of the brilliance of the author, cannot account for all of the variables in breeding programs, sports involvement, activities or historic uses for dogs.

3. The Number of Breedings Limit.

The list doesn't stop with the first two, but continues. Some of the legislation, while mandating that virtually all dogs be spayed or neutered, then provides for litter limits. Now I am not the brightest person on the planet, but it occurred to me the first time I read one of those legislative proposals that someone needed to take a course in basic biology. If all of the dogs are spayed and neutered, they... will... not... be... having... any... litters!!! OK, so forget that reality. Let's assume that regardless of the biology involved that the dog owner or breeder decides to pursue their passion of pure bred dogs anyway. Most of the legislation appears to limit the breeding to one litter a year at the most and two or three litters during the dog's life time.

The problem is quite obvious to those participating in the variety of dog hobbies available to dog lovers. If you breed a litter, what constitutes a litter? Some breedings do not take, and although the dog is bred, there are no puppies. And the size of a litter varies from one to 10 or occasionally more, with an average of about 5 puppies. Are all litters equal, or should we move into limiting the number of puppies? And what happens if a small litter is followed by a large litter which exceeds the limit by, say, 2 puppies? What do we do with those two? Should we just arbitrarily kill them or donate them to the government as a fine for exceeding the arbitrary limit? Yes, there are problems with the whole concept.

And there are more problems. In the real world of breeding, there are two kinds of dogs: Dogs (referring to males) and bitches (referring to females). Most legislation sets an arbitrary limit without regard to the sex of the dog. While most bitches are seldom bred on consecutive heats, they will then only produce one litter a year. But males can sire a dozen or more litters a month with no adverse health effects. But then, most males do not get to reproduce at all in the real world of pure bred dogs, for they are not superstars in their world of competition and no other bitch owner will be calling for their services. The superstar will get all of the calls, but if he is limited by legislation to one breeding per year, we have a major problem in the breed. We either have to select a lesser male or not breed.

Well I do think this could lead to an interesting market, where those who do not breed sell their right to breed to the superstar owner so they then have the carbon credits, er, excuse me, breeding credits to avoid violation of the law. Oh forget it. Cap and trade will not work any better than breed and trade will. It is all an illusionary creation of unnecessary intervention of well-meaning but misdirected political power.

4. The Trap of Non-uniform Ordinances.

Dog shows and sporting events have one thing in common. They are held at various locations across the country so that all of the participants and enthusiasts can participate. This means that dogs travel. They may take as few as two or three trips within a given state a year or as many as 52 weekends a year in multiple states. The dog exhibiting business is huge and contributes millions of dollars each year to the locations where shows are held. The problem for exhibitors is knowing what the regulations are in various states, counties, cities and other political subdivisions. The ordinances are not uniform, nor are they enforced with equal vigor.

I have yet to see an ordinance that exempts nonresident dogs who are in the territory covered by the ordinance temporarily for an event. Most exhibitors are troubled by stories circulating through their subculture of show dogs confiscated, euthanized or neutered against their will. But what would keep an overzealous enforcement officer from applying the letter of the law in a situation where it was not intended? Nothing. I served in law enforcement for many years, usually in a training capacity, and one of the things that always was high on my list of concerns was the officious officer looking for a violation without regard to the purpose and intent of the law. It happens. It happens far too often.

So breed clubs are faced with the possibility, even the probability, that some official in their parks department will issue an event permit for a dog competition without knowing that they are supporting and giving license to something that is not permitted in the city, county or state. Even more probable, is that unwitting officials are entrapping exhibitors into a setting where their unknowing violation of an anti-dog law will bring the enforcement personnel into the 'fish in a barrel' setting.

We could go on to describe the nature of the conflict that is predictably coming from the overreaching ordinances that threaten to kill a subculture of pet-enjoyment and stop their activities. And all of this potential for conflict is coming into focus through the efforts of a new and rising animal rights culture that is not dealing with the real issues at a grass roots level but is starting at the top: eliminate pets as personal

34

property, stop breeding of animals carte blanch, and replace the culture of animal sports with veganism. This is not a casual observation, but possibly a prophecy: The war is coming to a community near you.

Chapter Four

Defining "Puppy Mill"

Following one of the legislative hearings in our state, one of the senators asked a group of breeders to define for him what a puppy mill is. The question was sincere, and the frustration he was facing was obvious. He wanted a definition; he wanted to go after and stop the puppy mills, while leaving the hobby breeders alone.

I thought about it for some time and then explained to him that I could not help him. I did not have a definition. The presentation by the HSUS paid lobbyist in the session had been discredited, but I was left without a definition also. The paid lobbyist had presented two series of photos of two separate puppy mills in Nevada. The conclusion was that we had to stop puppy mills before they moved into our rural state and started taking over and shipping their mistreated puppies everywhere. We were in danger of becoming the puppy mill capitol of the world.

Fortunately, a young man in the gallery had heard the paid lobbyists presentation before, had gotten the pictures off of the presentation brochure and looked into them. The first one was of a puppy mill in Northern Nevada, off of Red Rock Road, near Stead. The source of the pictures was a place reported to Washoe County Animal control, a puppy mill with terrible animal abuse practices. What the official investigation revealed was a fox hound breeder who held hunts (field trial competitions) in the open spaces near the location where people came regularly with their dogs, horses and families to enjoy a weekend in the sun, camping out together and having their field trials. The facilities were immaculate and no abuse was happening. The reported size of the operation was estimated from pictures taken during one of the trials. At the time of the HSUS presentation, the kennel had moved out of state and no longer existed.

The second puppy mill was a clandestine operation in rural Nye County where a large fence and gates kept the HSUS representative from getting detailed photos. But, we were assured, there was a lot of traffic at the site and this was a major operation. So the young man also contacted the Nye County Sheriff who went ballistic. His report back showed that he recognized the photo, and it was not a dog breeding operation at all. It had been, in the past, a shelter for exotic animals, but had moved their operation into the Las Vegas area some years ago. They had been licensed, inspected by the Nye County Animal Control officer, and there was no abuse. And there were no dogs.

The young man had further presented current pictures of the sites, confirming that they were the same sites but in different time frames. His conclusion: There are no puppy mills, as defined by the paid HSUS lobbyist, and the whole presentation was a sham.

But, regardless of the sensationalism that distorts the issue for the sake of passing legislation, the question remains: What is a puppy mill? We have seen them on TV news magazines and seen the horrible conditions. If they are not in Nevada, then where are they? More, how do we control them or put them out of business?

But the question was not, where are they, but what are they? Until we can define what they are, it is going to be difficult to structure legislation to target them without arbitrarily targeting the family pet owner or the legitimate hobby breeder. And there is the crux of the matter.

Many years ago I was asked to attend a seminar on counseling, and to participate in a personality test that the seminar proposed would be useful in counseling. The personality test offered over 100 questions with multiple choice answers. We were instructed to choose the answer that best 'fit' and to disregard all the others. I think I was the only one in the class who decided that there were many questions where several of the answers might apply to me at a given time and that I could not make a yes or no decision about the question. I failed! The concluding profile explained that the entire human race fell into four basic personality types and that once you determined what the individual was, it would explain their attitudes, behavior and personality. Right!

It was a passing fad and before long most professionals decided that it was impossible to place the entire human race into four basic classifications. 40,000 maybe, but not 4. The human race is an infinitely complex species with differences that morph from one to another in millions of ways, and our personalities may not remain the same from year to year. It was an oversimplification that was useless at best and harmful at worst.

As I thought about defining a 'puppy mill', I thought of this earlier experience. If we were to decide on a number of dogs produced, whatever that number, it would be arbitrary. It would not define a difference between good and evil. We have friends who produce a ton of dogs because of their breeding system. They sell dogs on a co-ownership basis. This is a permitted classification by AKC and several other registries in which the owner keeps the dog and it lives with them, but the co-owner has certain contractual rights. In the case of our friends, they agree with the new owners that they (the breeder) can breed the bitches and take back the first litter or a part of several litters or some other breeding advantage. The end result is that their breeding relationships are spread over a lot of people who become co-breeders with them. Total number of puppies each year? I have no idea, but it is far more than my own and probably would raise the eyebrows of legislators anywhere. Yet, there is no abuse; all the puppies and breeding stock end up living in homes and facilities where they get individual love and care. So, what is the problem? If the owners default on the contract, the dog goes back to the primary breeder and not to a shelter. This operation has found a market for their dogs and has increased their kennel name across the nation, but are they a puppy mill? In terms of kennel conditions, animal care, pet socialization and love, or any other category of concern for these animals - there is really no issue. Except, if you set a number defining a puppy mill, it would no doubt apply.

Let's look at another operation. This operation I have not personally visited, but have talked to others who have. It is in the rural Midwest. It purchases dogs of various breeds from breeders. It sets standards for the breeders and inspects their kennels. When the puppies are purchased they are examined by a veterinarian, placed in holding kennels, given proper care, food and supervision. They are then distributed to pet stores and brokers across the nation with guarantees. The trucks are heated/ air conditioned, and the entire operation is inspected by the USDA. It has so far always met or exceeded their standards. The puppies are sold to homes, and presumably enjoy a healthy life in a good American family. Is there a problem here?

Well, there is for me. I could not do this. I want to control my breeding decisions and the quality of the product I am responsible for. I could not be a wholesaler and purchase random litters. Further, I could not allow a retail store to place my puppies in homes without the new owner being investigated and their home inspected. The first operation I described are friends, and I have done business with them. The second I could not do business with. But, given that they have clean and safe facilities and a market for their product, are they a puppy mill that needs to be shut down? Emotionally, I would argue that I do not like what they do, but could I sponsor legislation to shut them down? No, I could not, for the whole issue of any arbitrary numbers is missing the point. The real issue for us as a community in a political arena of responsibility is not to control the market, but to control the condition. If the puppies are safe and placed in good homes, then legally there should not be an issue, regardless of how I feel about the operation.

So, I have come to a conclusion about defining a puppy mill! There is no definition that can provide a legitimate argument for legislation. The issue is level of care and absence of abuse, and that cannot be arrived at by setting a number.

I watched our country officials work through this issue and start with a number of 100 puppies a year. No breeder in our area objected because no one could ever conceive of breeding 100 puppies. So it went to committee, where it became 50 puppies. Then it was reconsidered and became 5 litters a year, still a huge amount for any hobby breeder. And it continued to change until it became three litters. So what is the problem with this limit? Should everyone in town breed three litters a year? I mean, after all, can you imagine how crowded our shelters would be?

Well, I can imagine that there will be people who have no clue as to what they are doing, breeding litters of either pure bred dogs or mixed breed dogs and trying to make a profit on it. I can

40

also imagine them getting stuck with a yard full of puppies, a mail box full of veterinary bills and deciding to never do that again. This is the reality of bad backyard breeding. But those arbitrary limits will not address this problem, for it is one litter here and another there, and a shelter drop off in between. Regulating the hobby breeder who has a market and a return policy does nothing for the shelter and does not address the issue.

The issue is the welfare of the puppies, not the numbers. It has been four years since we had our last litter. We are planning one later this year or next and then may not breed again for several more years. We have ended up with three puppies returned in 55 years. Those dogs lived out their lives with us and never saw a shelter.

I certainly do not have an answer for all of the issues that are presented by animals in our culture. I do affirm that animals are important to people, and may even be a necessary part of human life. I also know that there is a legislative mind set in much of our government that supposes that all problems can be fixed by legislation; that government is obligated to do so. If this were the case then the proliferation of legislation over the years would have significantly solved most human problems. In that it has not, I rest my case.

Chapter Five

Fixing All the Problems

There is a supposition at the foundation of our nation that we have moved so far from, there may not be a road back. Here are some of those concepts from the founding fathers themselves:

"The Constitution is not an instrument for the government to restrain the people, it is an instrument for the people to restrain the government - lest it come to dominate our lives and interests." Patrick Henry

Is life so dear, or peace so sweet, as to be purchased at the price of chains or slavery? Forbid it, Almighty God! I know not what course others may take but as for me; give me liberty or give me death!" Patrick Henry

"Guard with jealous attention the public liberty. Suspect everyone who approaches that jewel. Unfortunately, nothing will preserve it but downright force. Whenever you give up that force, you are inevitably ruined." Patrick Henry

Because power corrupts, society's demands for moral authority and character increase as the importance of the position increases. John Adams

A wise and frugal government, which shall leave men free to regulate their own pursuits of industry and improvement, and shall not take from the mouth of labor the bread it has earned - this is the sum of good government. Thomas Jefferson

Experience hath shown, that even under the best forms of government those entrusted with power have, in time, and by slow operations, perverted it into tyranny. Thomas Jefferson

History affords us many instances of the ruin of states, by the prosecution of measures ill suited to the temper and genius of their people. The ordaining of laws in favor of one part of the nation, to the prejudice and oppression of another, is certainly the most erroneous and mistaken policy. Benjamin Franklin

As a man is said to have a right to his property, he may be equally said to have a property in his rights. Where an excess of power prevails, property of no sort is duly respected. No man is safe in his opinions, his person, his faculties, or his possessions. James Madison

If, from the more wretched parts of the old world, we look at those which are in an advanced stage of improvement, we still find the greedy hand of government thrusting itself into every corner and crevice of industry, and grasping the spoil of the multitude. Invention is continually exercised, to furnish new pretenses for revenues and taxation. It watches prosperity as its prey and permits none to escape without tribute. Thomas Paine

These are men who had experienced the long arm of British rule and had decided that it had lasted long enough to lose its reason and its soul. They distrusted government and its general tendency to expand and to place its finger of rule into every arena of the people. The founding fathers constructed a national philosophy which prevented government from entering the details of our lives by specifying what our rights are, which are given by God, and the constitutional limits of government.

It was never proposed that the law should not protect people from other people or that wrongs should not be righted. What it proposed was that the governmental frame of power should be restricted so that all power did not ultimately accrue to governmental administration. The rest of human life was designed to be free from control and governed by tort laws that had to do with a civil process in courts without criminal law or governmental policy.

During our last legislative session, I attended a meeting in which a county official offered as an explanation for the proposed ordinance, that the county had laws regarding kennels and numbers of animals in residential areas but that breeding had not been covered. My question was, why does it need to be covered? His answer floored me. It was that a state audit of some sort had determined that the county had not covered this area and that legal coverage was mandated. In other words, the activities of the citizenry had not been fully prescribed, so the county had to put forth the effort to be sure that all areas of human activity were covered by legislation.

I was at first dumbfounded by the concept, then frightened as many other citizens in the meeting accepted the explanation and gave aid and advice to the county official on how to provide that coverage. I am not sure what frightened me more; the presumption of government that all bases and activities must be covered, or the willingness of the other citizens in the meeting to accept that explanation.

I am not saying we do not need rules of behavior to protect animals, but I am saying to the degree that those rules move beyond the arena of animal abuse, they are part and parcel of the tyranny our forefathers warned us about. To conclude that freedom under government is defined as freedom to obey what rulers say, is to define away freedom altogether. Freedom is not and was never defined as freedom to shut up, sit down and obey. *It was defined as the absence of governmental dictate.* It was the definition of human rights as being superior to governmental rule and beyond governmental responsibility. It defined that sacred area of God given life and liberty into which government may not step.

Civil law was the court of appeal for interpersonal conflict. The sense of civil process was a logical and sound-minded judge or a jury of our peers would reach an amicable conclusion where public offense was concerned. So, if my animals are a nuisance to my neighbor because of smell or sound, then the civil process could determine my liability and fault, and order a means of correcting the offense. But the focus should remain on the offense - the smell and the noise - not on the presence of the animals alone.

But what has happened in our culture with the shift from the rural farm to the city setting, we have moved more and more jurisdiction from the civil side of the system to the criminal side of the system, outlawing freedom altogether. Conflict between people then, has become a matter of right and wrong rather than a relational issue of how we get along with equal freedoms.

Now, if you are following me, this leads to today's interjection into our legislative arena of laws and criminal penalties for a person to own a pet and enjoy some semblance of joy born in our agricultural roots, but increasingly outlawed in our modern culture. Front row and center is the paid lobbyist of PETA and HSUS and others, who determinedly insist that they have the right to tell the rest of the world how to conduct their homes and hobbies from the criminal bench.

I really do not care what the diet of the people involved with animal rights is, nor should they care about mine. I do not care if they will not have a domestic animal in the confinement of their yard, but I do care if they legislate against mine. I do not care what they do with their freedoms and lives unless they dedicate their energies and money to destroy mine. I do care, however, that there are millions of dollars raised to help the poor little abused puppies and kittens, and none of it goes to any hands-on care for the object used in fund raising advertising. That seems to me to be dishonest and criminal.

Passing legislation will not cure the human heart or alter our fallen state. Legislation will not fix all problems, restore human dignity or stimulate the economy. Legislation cannot do everything or solve all problems, nor should it try. And that is the primary message of our forefathers - "Do these things only and let people solve the rest of their problems and live their own lives." You DO NOT HAVE TO COVER ALL THE BASES! And if you believe you should, you are not the friend of the people - you are the enemy.

Chapter Six

The War is Here!

No need to wait, there is a war available near you now.

I remember getting up one morning, some years ago and turning on the news, which is always my morning ritual. I seldom listen to it, just glance at the weather, and grab a shower and some toast and head out the door. But on this day they kept showing an airplane flying into a building, so I stopped to watch. Then in the middle of the broadcast another plane flew into the adjoining tower. It took me some time to assimilate what was happening, as it did those on the news media I was watching. I remember that day, and it will be emblazoned on my aging mind as long as I live.

Well, it is happening again. No not airplanes and towers and such national issues - in that sense there is no parallel - but the shock and emotion is there none-the-less. All this week I have been preparing position papers and driving to the halls of local and state government to testify on some of the most gosh-awful legislation I have ever seen. It is an all-out war.

I was told by another dog person working with our team that 147 pieces of legislation are pending right now in 37 states across the nation. Although each have different wording depending on which politician wrote and presented them, they all have the same emphasis behind them and the signature objectives of HSUS, the Humane Society of the United States.

Can you believe that this nation-wide campaign happened without their announcing it to us? I mean, there should be some ethical agreement in warfare; if you are going to go to war you should declare war beforehand to give us a chance to prepare! Right? Well, they did their job well, and their preemptive strike has been devastating. This has to go down as the Pearl Harbor of Dogdom.

My involvement sort of evolved from knowing there was a problem and seeing Stormy Hope become our German Shepherd Dog Club of America, Committee Chair for Legislative Affairs. Then I watched her take off, I mean like General Patton after a coward. Next thing I knew she was asking our club to appoint regional committee members to serve with her, and since we have a grand total of four local members (two of which are married to the other two) I was on the hook.

I used to get about 100 emails a day from various sources, but all of a sudden I was getting double that number. The material was pouring in, and I was made aware of something happening on a national scale. Then, there it was, legislation not trickling in from one place or another, but pouring in from all over the nation. Frankly, I was overwhelmed and had no idea what to do. That soon changed. My state, Nevada – the rough and rugged capitol of the west with its gun toting, rugged individualists – had proposed anti-breeder legislation, and I had to do something. Then our whole county followed with many – 'don't leave us out of the fun' – ordinances.

I scurried around to get the drafts of the laws and ordinances, and started writing and sending emails to each of the legislators and commissioners, though I thought it might be all for naught. Then Stormy sent me an email about a group in our state simply calling themselves NV DOG LAW, so I emailed them and got on their email list. It appeared there were 6 or 8 all breed dog people

48

who had gotten together when I joined, but within a couple of weeks the group had grown to a sizable membership.

I went down to the Capitol to testify against the bill, and there in the meeting I met my first real live HSUS paid lobbyist. She was rather pretty and charming. My casual inspection did not reveal any horns or pitchfork, although I was certain they were well concealed under her professional business attire. The committee meeting began and the bill was presented by the Senator who did such things. The HSUS lady testified in favor of the bill, citing all kinds of statistics to show that there were horrid conditions in my kennel, and that I was profiting from the misery of all the neglected puppies I was breeding to dump on the local shelter. She cited facts and figures to prove beyond a doubt that breeders were evil and more dogs were killed every year than there were dollars in the stimulus bill. I started to be amazed at the size of the problem this legislation was going to stop, and then I realized where the horns and pitchfork had been concealed – in her tongue.

Well, there were 6 or 7 people there to testify in opposition to the bill, and if I do say so myself, we did a pretty fair job. The President of the Nevada Veterinary Association testified, disputing the facts and figures with his own facts and figures, concluding that the HSUS statistics must have been manufactured. He did not say anyone was lying, but I did see the cute little well-dressed HSUS lobbyist slip out during his conclusion.

It did not end there. That preliminary meeting was followed by the formal hearing just a few days later. What happened there was absolutely amazing. The HSUS lady had managed to rally two other people to testify with her about the terrible conditions of animals and the evils of breeding. The committee listened, but the atmosphere was different this time. This time, they asked questions about the statistics and the need for some of the specifics of the proposed legislation.

During their questioning I turned to see who was left in the room and found the committee chambers packed out, wall to wall/ standing room only with an overflow crowd in the hall. These people were not professional lobbyists, but casually dressed people from farms, ranches and breed clubs from all over the state. Some had driven up to 300 miles to be there. We had raised an army in just a few weeks without the help of full time staff or a big supporting budget.

When they asked for those who were going to testify against the legislation to come up, half the crowd stood. The chairman asked three people to come first, one being the President of the Veterinary Association, one being the President of the Livestock Association and the other the Head of the Nevada Department of Agriculture. The Agriculture chief went first, telling them he wanted nothing to do with this legislation and if they passed it, his department would not administer it. They had no funds, no time and he was not going to send his people out door to door snooping in fellow Americans' windows and yards. The audience erupted in applause and cheers, which brought the committee chairman's gavel pounding on the table. He threatened us soundly, but the point was made.

After those three testified, a breeder of Kelpies came up and started methodically working through each of the statistics previously presented by the HSUS paid lobbyist. She with grace and force blew them away. She talked for about 20 minutes, and in the end, there was nothing more to be said. It was covered. I gave a short synopsis, and left it to the committee. One Senator commented, "Well, this is dead."

I was amazed that what HSUS had initiated, clearly to destroy us, had instead simply awakened a sleeping giant. I really didn't know there were so many breed enthusiasts in our area, but they all came together, formed email networks, worked on wording and presentations and simply overwhelmed the proposed bill with sound arguments and real facts. I was never so proud to be called a breeder in my life.

So I am not as intimidated any longer. It is not a task for one, but for an army, and the soldiers are there, in various breeds and places in the community, ready to defend their passion and to protect the dogs they love and the sports they have chosen. I think ultimately we are going to win this war, and our enemy, who chose to make us the enemy before we knew it was happening, will be sorry they started it!

But that is not the end of the story. A few week later it was reported that the dead bills were forwarded to the House committee. In a private session, late one night, attended by the HSUS Lobbyist, the bills were attached to a dog-fighting bill (which everyone favored) sent to the house and senate, and got it approved without discussion or public hearing. I asked a couple of legislators later why they did that, but they did not even know what was in the amendments. They were just trying to stop any dog fighting rings in our state.

I've been told there are two things you never want to know: How sausages and legislation is made. As for legislation, I am now a certified cynic. I hold out much better hope for sausages.

The following is a chart of definitions showing the difference between the Animal Rights Agenda and the position of those who are in favor of Animal Welfare as an alternative:

Animal Welfare Vs Animal Rights

Animal Welfare Activists' Beliefs:

- *We seek to improve the treatment and well-being of animals.*
- We support the humane treatment of animals that ensures comfort and freedom from unnecessary pain and suffering.
- We have the right to "own" animals -- they are our property.
- We believe animal owners should provide loving care for the lifetime of their animals.

Animal Rights Activists' Beliefs are:

- *They seek to end the use and ownership of animals.*
- They believe any use of an animal is exploitation so, not only must we stop using them for food and clothing, but pet ownership must be outlawed as well.
- They want to obtain legal rights for animals as they believe animals and humans are equal.
- They use false and unsubstantiated allegations of animal abuse to raise funds, attract media.
- They want to gain attention and bring supporters into the movement. (*The Inhumane Crusade*, Daniel T. Oliver)

The Twelve Steps of the Animal Rights Agenda
("The Politics of Animal Liberation," by Kim Bartlett, Editor of Animals' Agenda, November 1987.)

1. Abolish by law all animal research.
2. Abolish by law all other types of animal testing.

3. Encourage vegetarianism for ethical, ecological, and health reasons.

4. Phase out intensive confinement livestock production.

5. Eliminate use of herbicides, pesticides, etc.

6. Transfer animal law enforcement of Department of Agriculture to another agency.

7. Eliminate commercial trapping and fur ranching.

8. Prohibit hunting, trapping and fishing for sport.

9. Urge U.S. action to prevent destruction of rainforests and end international trade in wildlife and goods produced from exotic and/or endangered fauna or flora.

10. Discourage any further breeding of companion animals, including pedigreed or purebred dogs and cats. Promote spay and neuter of all pets by government subsidized clinics.

11. End the use of animals in entertainment and sports, with reappraisal of zoos and aquariums.

12. Prohibit genetic manipulation of species.

Chapter Seven

Freedom & Control – The Continuum

For over 20 years I taught one class a semester at the community college in the Criminal Justice Department. My service in police work and training seemed to give a great foundation for explaining to aspiring law enforcement officers the way it really is.

I started the first class of each semester with a statement that always brought a mixed reaction. I would shout, "Crime is a solvable problem!" Inevitably a student or two would disagree so strongly as to speak up and the argument was on. My follow-up questions was:

Is there any nation or society in the world today or at any time in history that had a lower crime rate than we do in our nation today?

After a thoughtful pause, there would always be an affirmative answer – of course there is and was. So the question that followed was, "How did they achieve their lesser crime rate?" And the answer was always the same: By increasing enforcement, making stricter laws and increasing the police force – the means of control.

Some years ago my wife went to China on a shopping junket with a group of ladies. They went to Hong Kong, China, Japan and Korea, starting with only a small cosmetic bag and coming home with... Well, you can only guess what they brought home. But the most remarkable part of the trip was not in the bargains they found but in the shock at seeing how other cultures lived. They remarked about the claims of China that they had very little crime, but it was obvious why. There were police and soldiers on every street corner with automatic weapons, and others patrolling the blocks in between. Of course they had little crime because they had high control.

There are still some cultures that cut off the hand of the thief, stone the adulterer, shoot those who disagree with the government and in general create terror within their borders. We, I've always argued, can do the same and stop or drastically reduce our crime rate and greatly reduce our prison population. But when I would propose that solution to my class, they would always react with rejection of the idea. They have learned to enjoy their freedom and to reject strong control.

The point of this class and of this chapter is to underscore the continuum that exists between freedom and control. They are equal opposites on the same continuum and are interactive on that continuum. The more control, the less freedom. The more freedom we enjoy, the less control there has to be. That being so, we choose our crime rate, and we choose our level of freedom. We decide whether to stop misbehavior which inevitably limits our freedom to act by our own conscience and volition. You can't have it both ways. As we move along that line of action and reaction, increasing control or freedom will have an effect on the other.

The illusion of those who deal in law is that we can ultimately solve all human problems by enacting an ordinance to specify what human behavior should be. But in doing so, there are several presumptions that follow:

1. We assume we have the right to do so.
2. We assume we are wise enough to do so.

3. We are, by our very act of bringing control, passing judgment on some form of human behavior as evil and worthy of being prohibited.
4. We are choosing to reduce freedom based on the assumption we cannot trust human behavior and self determination.
5. We are weighting the behavior targeted with some penalty that would not exist if people were free to determine their own behavior.
6. We are assuming common sense is unavailable and the family, community, club or social substructure in which the behavior exists, is incapable of bringing social control (informal direction) without legal action (formal control).

The argument is often advanced by those who deal in making laws that this one more act of control is essential to public safety or harmony and that this is not a conspiracy of control. But those who experience the annual process of building more social constraints feel the effects of not just more constraint and the loss of freedom but of the cost of making the laws, enforcing the laws, punishing the people who have violated them and the whole culture of criminal justice.

It does not have to be an organized conspiracy to control; it is simply the end result of movement along the continuum. It is a slippery slope as any activity for the sake of increased freedom or increased control moves the balance point along the line. There are no inconsequential actions that have no effect when dealing with this continuum. For each action on the line, there is an equal and opposite reaction. Maybe we could call this the physics of social action.

There are many evils in the human family. People are seldom in agreement as to what is right, sensible, and moral or of value. We all probably laugh regularly at the stupidity of some human behavior we hear about or see on TV. The human race is awash in a plethora of incidents that betray ignorance, stupidity or just plain meanness. There is no end to the imagination of the genius or the ignorant. The problem is in determining what to do about it.

Once we decide we should do something about it, however, we have to understand the consequences of the inevitable effects our regulations have on the freedom of others. Law not only has consequences to the evildoer, but also to those who are caught in the letter of the law without having been the target of the law. There are always unintended consequences. The greatest of these is that the whole of our culture loses freedom in the decision to bring greater control. You cannot do one without the other. The growing philosophy of government in many areas is all activities need to be categorized and either permitted by government or regulated with some sort of licensure, or prohibited. For government to be absent from any arena of life seems inexcusable to those with this mindset. But it is precisely that mindset that moves our society along that continuum of freedom and control toward the tyranny of control. Whither it is intended or not, it is an interactive balance that moves with each act of legislation. Good people with seemingly noble motives can exact control as inflexibly as the evil despot.

So, how then shall we determine where the balance point will be? Which do we value more, the safety of control or the freedom to make our own choices? These are not easy matters, for no one that I know would seriously argue for anarchy. We would probably all agree we need some government and there is a legitimate function for a police force that protects our communities. But shall we become like other cultures where they do not have freedom to determine their own destiny?

This current legislative session has found animal legislation springing up across the land in a seemingly orchestrated move to bring severe control and even determine limits on the choices people have as to the kind of pet, the number of pets and whether or not people have the right to even perpetuate their animal breed. By one count there are 147 pieces of animal legislation being proposed in 37 states. Most of these are primarily aimed at limiting reproduction of pets and the kinds of pets we are allowed to own. All of them shift the decision-making that has traditionally been with the pet owner, to the state. All presume the state is wiser and better able to make decisions than we are. All presume a problem needs a that needs a solution, and all move us along the axis of freedom and control with an objective to solve problems by formal means rather than by allowing informal relationships to influence our lives and neighborhoods. The major problem with this push is the assumption that all problems need to be solved, and legislation is the solution.

What will happen, with the balance between freedom and control, is being determined for us who love animals. It is more than an argument; it is a decision. The problem is, we have become a nation with a deep history and 233 years of legislatures making decisions to define how much control, and consequently, how much freedom we will enjoy. Too often, I suspect, those functions have gone on as business as usual without any understanding that, in the passing of thousands of laws each year, we as a nation have not only regulated evils we have defined, but also removed from the populace the freedom to decide much of anything for themselves.

God bless America, land that I love, and God protect us from those who would save us from ourselves.

Chapter Eight

The Law of Progressive Density

The value of the diamond is not in that it is made of carbon but that it has been crystallized into a density many times greater than its original component material. Time and pressure tends to create density. This is not just true in the formation of gemstones, but it is also true in social structures. The longer a group exists, the greater its social structures.

We see this law in motion in our government and, in my opinion, it has almost reached critical mass. Here is how it happens. The founders of this nation came here for several reasons. They came for religious freedom, for the opportunity to get away from the confines of an old and tight country and for the adventure that this new land afforded them. They started with nothing more than the common law which was loosely based on broader ethical foundations, but which they interpreted anew in this grand new social experiment. The leaders of the day were employed in a variety of commercial ventures and volunteered their time to serve as the nation needed their attendance.

But we grew and we changed, and the law of progressive density took over without our ever knowing it. There were problems in our land that the Ten Commandments did not specifically address, so our leaders got together and made new laws, one here, one there and then some more. In the making of laws there was no end, so we decided to pay our leaders to be there full time. And what do you think they thought they were supposed to do? Make more laws, develop more programs and solve more problems. They, without understanding the dynamic they were sucked into, participated in the law of progressive density.

Time went on. There were more laws and more regulations that were not laws passed by our legislators. And since the law of progressive density is as it is, there was no time to make enough laws to cover the growing governmental bureaus that developed, so the leaders allowed them to make their own regulations as well as the penalties for not obeying them. Before long, those regulations for each governmental agency were so vast and powerful that they were greater in number than the laws passed by congress. Now, years later, the compounding of this subtle process gives us Federal Law, State Law, County Ordinances, City Ordinances, plus the regulations of HUD, IRS, CDC, DOA, USFS, DOE, USDA, and an endless list of acronyms no sane person knows or understands. Each has enough volumes of regulations and policies to keep the world warm through 100 future ice ages should we burn them for heat – which may not be a bad idea anyway.

The end result of this phenomenon of progressive legal density is, it is virtually impossible to step outside ones door in the morning without breaking some law or failing to comply with some bureaucratic regulation. The sheer weight of the density we have created is overpowering, and yet, unlike the diamond, it does not increase the value one bit. One of the powerful things that happens in this increase of regulation is the objective becomes smaller and more minute as time goes on. That is, we started with "Thou shalt not murder," an now we are down to, even if you planted the tree ten years ago, you have to have a permit and environmental clearance before you cut it down to do something on your own property. Really! I kid you not! Some communities tell you what color to paint your house, and where to park your car.

In that increased density of regulation, we have come to a time when a group of people, presumably interested in helping poor unfortunate animals, has decided the rest of us are ignorant fools who need more regulations concerning how to treat our animals, how many we can have and whether or not we are bright enough to breed them or not – with the current emphasis on NOT! You will not breed.

Now that our law against murder has worked so well (sarcasm intended), we turn our attention and efforts to the tremendous task of making legislation to control the mean and evil sorts who own animals and those ring leaders of animal abuse, the hobby breeders. The proliferation of legislation in our day is astounding. It is as though legislators were sitting around with nothing to do, someone threw them a 'regulation bone' and off they went in a feeding frenzy of "Ah, ha! Now we have something to do besides creating scandals."

Has it ever occurred to any one elected official that, number one, there is a line of common human decency past which leaders should not pass... You know like the bill of rights that suggests we are endowed by our creator with certain rights and were probably given sufficient brains to handle those rights and to pursue the fundamentals of life and liberty without some government rule, regulation or dictate to guide us?

Has it ever occurred to an elected official that, number two, just because one is elected to office does not necessarily mean one should find some new human activity that is unregulated and set government standards for it? How about you just go off to your capitol in Washington or where ever else you are going, and play golf for four years and leave me and my dogs the hell alone!

Let's suppose we have sufficient instincts and knowledge to live life and have good days without your permission or inspection! How on earth did our forefathers get by without everyone trying to save them from themselves and their animals?

Enough! Way 'over the top' enough!

Yes, I'm ticked – mad as a hornet! What on earth are we doing to our American dream? What is happening to our pursuit of happiness and the freedom that is supposed to attend it? For us who love our animals and who enjoy the finer pursuits of the sport of the purebred dog, the sky IS falling. City after city, county after county, and state after state is being led into the frenzy of a legislative euphoria, as though they were hooked on some mind-altering drug. Their goal is to see that their legislation is tighter than the one in the other jurisdiction. It is mind-boggling how apparently well-meaning leaders of a free society become those who think our freedom is dangerous to us and our neighbors.

I have a proposal: don't vote for anyone who says they are going to go to the capitol to solve problems and give us more benefits. Vote for the lazy candidate who says they are going to do nothing for us but eliminate more laws than their counterparts can pass. How about electing the guy or gal who promises to be absent from most legislative sessions, spending time on the streets with their constituency, playing pool and coaching little league.

The law of progressive density has done its work, and the pressure and time has compressed our freedom to own and breed our beloved dogs into a crystallized mass. But it doesn't smell like a diamond. It has the strange odor of a pile of refuse left by all the departing animals, running for their lives.

Let's stop this nonsense.

63

Chapter Nine

"Presentism" - Damn the Past

Academia has coined a new word, "presentism," to describe the phenomena of our propensity to forget the social contexts of the past and to interpret all of history and present propriety by the social conscience of our immediate worldview. Nowhere is that phenomenon more poignant than in the world of animals, pets and the sports surrounding the pure bred dog.

I was raised in a semi-rural setting, and Dad was an icon of the survivors of the Great Depression. He did not know about Green Peace or PETA or global warming, yet nothing went to waste in the quest for feeding the family and mere survival. We were a transitional family, so to speak, coming out of an agricultural setting into an industrial world where all the rules were different and the social order of things was changing – fast!

In the early 1900's 90+ % of our population lived on the family farm and raised their own food. My parents came from that setting, and making the transition into the industrial world involved more than just a trip to town. It required a change of mind set and schedule and, well, one's entire worldview. We kept animals and raised them for food. Everyone had chores, and mine was to feed the chickens, gather the eggs, determine which chickens were not laying and kill them for dinner. I never enjoyed the task, but I considered it a necessity of survival, so I did it. I also tended the rabbits and similarly killed them, skinned them and took the pelts to the man up the street who took them to market.

Our garden produced the rest of our food, along with those few items we bought from the store. Dad milked the cow and the goats, and mom worked herself silly tending to the domestic chores that kept the family in clothes, home-cooked food and minor medical attention.

I never felt unfortunate, for all of the neighbors lived similarly and traded with us for our milk, cheese, vegetables and eggs. It was a way of life. Reality, as we knew it, was defined, not by a philosophical dictate, but by the necessities of living.

I look back with fond memories, although I have no intention of going back to the icebox, wringer washers, cars that break down and no TV. While socially I am not sure if the world is better, technologically it is vastly better. The problem is not in the changes that have taken place but in our loss of a sense of history, our failing memory of times gone by. While I understand the relationship we had with the land and the animals, our present world has no sense of that era, and, in fact, has decided it should not have been as it was. Let me explain...

Our mania is for a radical sort of "presentism": the belief the actions and actors of the past should be evaluated, and usually condemned, by present-day standards. For some reason, the 'live-and-let-live' of past generations seems to have given rise to absolutes forced on others. Presentism not only wants to judge the past by the criteria of the present, but fails to have any historical imagination and can't conceive the future being radically different from today. Images of the future seem to be extrapolations of the limited present with no consideration of the past, of life before our complex now.

But what of our future? If the PETA imperative were to be our future and a new century find us living in a world in which no one who is law abiding would dare to eat an animal, or kill it, or skin it, or fence it in, or worse – proclaim ownership of it – what would our world look like, and how would it look back on our agricultural past? And how would that world think of the dogs on lead, running around the ring at Westminster Kennel Club?

I wonder if the gallery of villains of the past will include my name in infamy along with Colonel Sanders, Ronald McDonald, Oscar Mayer, and the President of the AKC? Will 'PETA-like' uniformed agents usher us into the 22nd century's version of the Orwell's 1984, where our agricultural past leaves the memory of our zoos and farms classified historically with shame? Will the newspapers of the future have to issue public apologies in the next century for having run ads for puppies for sale?

While our public officials have labored hard to remove from our culture any sign of the old teachings of Eugenics, it has no problem deciding that one breed of dog should be declared vicious and eliminated from breeding. To be consistent, I wonder why wouldn't the science of genetics in one species be the same as when applied to another species? If people are animals/ animals are people wouldn't eliminating one species be as appalling as Eugenics?

It seems strange to me to read of the proliferation of public laws to limit humankind's relationship to animals and to see the animal in such drastically different proportions then did my parents. No one ever told Dad he could only have three chickens or no more than five total animals or could not plant a garden larger than the local markets produce isle. No one ever complained about his milk or his cheese – no one! No one decided for him the breed of cow he would have or the kind of

66

dog that would protect the farm. It was a different era and a different mindset.

How did it happen that one group of animal rights activists became a dozen or more and they, devoid of any issues of survival of their own have decided not only to alter everyone's present in relationship to our animals, but to revise our sense of the values of history as well? No, time has not always given us progress, but in some cases a retrograde process of over-control and legalized abuse. The activists spin is a presumed concern for the welfare of animals, which they think we in the animal sports do not have. And since that presumption includes our unwillingness to abide by their dictates and definitions, we will certainly pay for it by being the targets of impossible legislative demands.

Presentism is certainly alive and well in our land and if we are not careful, it will revise history and reality to damn us to the annals of infamy. They shall take my dog away from me, when they pry its leash out of my cold dead hand! I think I'll go join the NRA.

Chapter Ten

What's The Problem?

This coming year I shall mark an anniversary: 56 years with the German shepherd dog. I cannot imagine life without my ever present dog and the love shared through the years. Yet, increasingly my image in the world is changing. I used to be the country boy with the ever present dog, but these days I think I am supposed to hide the fact I breed dogs and keep multiple dogs at my house. Somehow, what started out to be a fun hobby and the fulfillment of a passion has become evil. I have dogs, I breed dogs and I sell dogs. I am, or so I am told, a major contributor to animal over-population and animal cruelty.

There is a gathering cloud in our land that is sweeping through city councils, county commissions and state legislatures. It is the assumption that someone has to put a stop to the evils of over-population and stop those evil sorts who breed and sell dogs. Certainly there is something demented in these people, we are told, who ignore the dogs already born and in need of homes to contribute to the problem by producing more.

Before I react too much, let me tell you about the 'animal cruelty' at our house. Each animal lover is different and has different facilities and needs, so I don't propose our situation as the standard everyone should use. Far be it from me to follow the dictates of those who propose they know best for my hobby and dogs by telling others I am the standard. But let me tell you none-the-less about our poor, mistreated dogs.

All of our puppies go to homes that I have personally inspected to determine the general atmosphere and safety of the setting. More than once I have returned from my inspection trip and sent a kind "thank you for applying but no thank you!" note to the prospective owner. No, I am quite selective in placing our dogs. When we do, there is a written note telling them that, as the breeder, I am responsible for this animal for life. If for any reason, throughout its lifetime, they need to part with it, they must agree to return the dog to me.

Ariel was a fine puppy, not quite what we would show in the ring, but of great temperament and brains. A lady came by who was in the early stages of Multiple Sclerosis, and her doctor had recommended she get a dog for companionship and for daily exercise. She loved Ariel. And Ariel loved her, so she went off to be a companion/therapy dog. I checked on her periodically, and at first everything was fine. Then as the disease become worse so did the depression that tormented this lady. One day the owner of the apartment complex where the lady and Ariel lived called to say there was a problem. She found Ariel in her yard without food or water.

I rushed to the apartment and found the lady, cloistered in her room with the blinds pulled, hiding in her bed, hoping to die. I roused her, got her up, fed and watered Ariel, cleaned the yard and made the lady go for a walk with Ariel and me. As we walked, we talked. She had enough money to buy groceries and dog food, and was able to move and walk, but was finding it increasingly difficult and painful to keep the muscles moving. Yet, she knew that she should and that she was responsible for Ariel. She had simply succumbed to the temptation to fear the eventualities of her disease rather than enjoying what she could of each day. She agreed to get counseling and to fight the depression. Ariel stayed for the moment.

I regularly went by to check on Ariel and the lady and to encourage her to keep going. Then another call came from the apartment manager informing me that Ariel needed me. She had gone by the apartment several times over a couple of days and Ariel was not in her yard. There were no signs of life. She assumed they had gone visiting the lady's children in California as they occasionally did, but on the morning of this call, she saw Ariel ripping the living room blinds down and banging loudly at the door. She called the police and got her pass key, entering to find the lady again in her bed. She had been there without food or water for the better part of the week and was dehydrated and near the death she was obviously seeking. She was rushed to the hospital, but Ariel needed help.

I arrived shortly after the call and fed and watered Ariel who appeared to be better off than her owner, then took her on home. I called her family and they agreed it was time for the lady to come live with them. Ariel had done her job. She had kept the lady as active as she could and helped her fight the depression as long as she could. In one final act of getting the attention her master needed, she had saved her life.

Ariel received a hero's reception when she came home, and she remains with us until this day. She will remain with us as the grey hair covers her chin and time shortens her stride and slows her pace. She deserves to rest now and relax in the sun and sleep on the bed. She has done her duty to human kind.

All of our dogs are spoiled. We are fortunate to have enough acreage that each pack has a fenced yard of an acre or so to run, and each has a doggy door into a section of the house. Each is fed the best food, gets a Meaty Bone before bed and goes for a long walk with us each day. None of our friends think there is any abuse here, and many want to believe in reincarnation, hoping to come back as one of our dogs.

Most of the breeders and show exhibitors we associate with have a similar stance. Their dogs go to forever homes, but if something happens, they take responsibility for the dog and either keep it or find it another home with the same arrangement. All of the exhibitors and show enthusiasts we associate with spoil their dogs. Now! What is wrong with this picture?

What is wrong, we are told, is that we produce more dogs when there are already too many abandoned dogs in the shelters that need homes. So, there needs to be legislation to stop the breeders so we eliminate the problem of over-population. Now understand, I have taken several dogs back over the years and none of them have ended up in a shelter. In fact, I do not know of any of my dogs who have been abandoned or ended up in a shelter. Yes, we have lost contact with some of the owners, so I have not been able to track every dog. But to my knowledge, none have been abandoned without our taking them back home to live out their life with love and lots of spoiling.

So, where is the problem? I do know dogs get abandoned. I do know we have a local shelter. I have been around our city enough to know those pockets of the city that have unconfined dogs running loose and breeding randomly. I've seen the people standing in front of the supermarket with the box of puppies who have not had their shots or been wormed, going out to random owners who may or may not know how to care for this unfortunate product of irresponsibility.

So let me get this straight... The well-meaning and well-financed animal rights people want to create legislation to stop me. This will have little or no effect on those who are

71

irresponsible and simply do not care enough to learn how to take care of their pets. I don't understand. Statistical evidence is already coming in showing the failure of these well-meaning, heart-wrenching legislative 'solutions.' They don't work. They don't work because they are not targeting the problem; they are targeting the answer. If everyone were responsible for their animals, then no legislation would be needed.

I do have a solution, but it is politically incorrect to advance it. I mean, rounding up the strays is admirable and sterilizing them is fine, but shouldn't we round up the irresponsible owners and sterilize… Oh forget it. I can't say that on TV.

Now there is a new challenge. The animal rights people have decided breeders are ruining the dog by creating and breeding specific breeds as opposed to allowing them to randomly breed. Let's see if I understand! The vast majority of dogs in the shelters are mixed breeds so the pure bred dog is not the real issue, but, we shouldn't breed them anyway because we create health issues? In other words, we should not breed and should not have pure bred sports and what – we should not have companion animals at all? Seems like that is the point doesn't it?

I have a friend who heads up the state Department of Wildlife here in Nevada. Their studies show that the Coyote here lives roughly an average of three years. Their life in the wild is limited by food supply, weather, disease and genetic problems passed on randomly. It certainly does not make sense that breeders who track the genetics of their breed and breed to improve health are doing a worse job than nature. That same argument applies to the random health issues of the mixed breed. Sure it is possible to advance a 'proof text' case of "my mixed breed lived to be 15 years old." But in general, nature does not necessarily take care of genetic predictions, studies and breeding decisions. Want more proof? Look at the human race.

I think it is time for us to unite our efforts with the agricultural communities and other interests who are being affected by this rush to legislate, and that we push back with fund raising and legislative proposals of our own. On second thought, let's just stop trying to solve the problems of human irresponsibility by legislating against the responsible. That makes sense to me.

This is not a plea to get rid of protective measures for our animals. Many animals are abused and abandoned, but what is happening is focusing on the problem of unwanted pets in shelters. This is the wrong target. Mixed breed animals, randomly bred because they are not tended to and are allowed to run loose and then find their way to the city pound are not addressed in current legislation. It is assumed that by passing a law against breeding, everyone will comply; this is without merit. The responsible will comply, but they are not the problem. We are focusing our legislative efforts on pet owners in general rather than focusing on the behavior of the irresponsible. Thus, the laws become more restrictive while the problem continues to grow.

Chapter Eleven

Where Have All the Animals Gone?

Thirty Seven percent of American homes include at least one dog. The dog has been the constant companion to man since the beginning of time, and it appears modern mankind has not altered their love for and reliance on their canine companions. Where dogs of prehistory were able to warn the cave dwellers of the approach of rival tribes and other dangers, today's dogs are no less valuable. Crime ravages American cities, and threatens every family today. In that sense, little has changed as dogs protect their owners.

But there have been changes. As we have discovered the superior senses and abilities of our canine population, we have increased their role in our lives. From the search of the rubble after 9-11-01 of the World Trade Center to the search and rescue efforts in Haiti, Chili, and other parts of the world, the majestic dog has served to save lives and work side by side with their human counterpart in detecting and relieving the pain of tragedy.

You cannot get on an airplane to travel today without owing a debt of gratitude to the dog who sniff searched the luggage for explosives before it went into the plane with you. The stories of dogs used in medicine to detect cancer, warn of an impending epileptic seizure, guide the blind, respond for the deaf, assist the crippled and so forth is common and legend.

Add to that the role of dogs in fire investigations, sniffing out accelerants, working with our military and police departments, comforting the ill and injured as therapy dogs, and a thousand kinds of security and beneficial activities, including sniffing out truffles and detecting spoiled produce and food products. The role of the dog has increased over time and through the shifting cultures of the humans on the planet.

Even in the day to day life of the pet owner, the lowly dog is beneficial. He encourages exercise and social contact and alters the mood of the depressed by his consistent love and affection. The pet owner will live a longer life than their non-dog counterpart, and, by all reports, enjoy it more. Pets have beneficial effects for people even if they do not perform heroic tasks.

But, not everyone loves pets nor believes they should be confined in the family yard. In recent years a wave of philosophic changes threaten to usher us into an entirely new cultural norm in which the animals are all returned to the wild and people are pet free. The emphasis does not stop there...

Traditional agricultural interests are also the target of this sweeping cultural change, or proposed change. The use of animals of any kind for meat, labor, milk and dairy products, leather or any use by humans whatsoever is under attack. And all of this is done with the ignorant cooperation of legislative bodies and elected officials who have no clue as to the broader philosophical scope of the issues. The illusion is, how can people and organizations who are concerned with the welfare of animals be deceitful and bad? But the question betrays the answer. No one, including the dog clubs, dog registries, shelters and agricultural interests is against animal welfare. That is not the issue. The issue is ANIMAL RIGHTS, clear and simple.

I have been heavily involved with animals all of my life and I have no tolerance for animal abuse - None - Zero! I do not know a breeder or owner or farmer who has any tolerance for those who abuse animals. Yet, the animal-owning culture is under extreme scrutiny and attack, and is being portrayed as the evil side of darkness that needs to be controlled and legislated against.

The driving force for this phenomenon is not the legislators who pass the laws, not in large part. The driving force is a planned philosophical program of proposed laws, which are incrementally released year by year into legislative bodies across the nation with coordinated efficiency by those who propose to speak for the animals and protect the poor abused innocent creatures of the planet. It all sounds good, but the end result is clearly to eliminate animals for human companionship and use altogether.

Laws requiring mandatory spay and neutering of all pet animals will have the effect, if enforced and obeyed, of eliminating the entire pet population within the life span of this generation of pets. Already registrations of pure bred dogs have fallen in recent years to astonishing lows, and if those trends continue, AKC and many other registries will soon be nonexistent. Some breeds are already nearing extinction, and yet there is no outcry from the environmental extremists to save the breeds. The continuous cry for more restrictive legislation continues. It is not generated by those who are living with the animals and who support animal welfare laws and their enforcement. It is the result of a concerted effort by several large organizations who are philosophically committed to Animal Rights.

Animal Rights is not related to animal welfare in any form either philosophically or in practice. It is a totally separate issue emanating from separate camps, and there is no avenue for cooperation. They are different culturally, philosophically and organizationally. The entire animal world is under attack from those who, at the core of their belief system want to eliminate any human oversight and use of animals. From the agricultural culture of the past, stands the honorable and straightforward farmer type, with family values and strong ties to the community, the family and his animals. On the other side is a whole new way of thinking in which elitist organizations and people propose to be saving the animals from people who own them by setting them free, giving them their own rights and removing them from the protection of being private property in an ownership relationship with people.

If AR goals are accomplished, these organizations and their rulers will be setting the agenda for animals and defining their role in our lives, without ownership or immediate contact. They will determine whether agricultural interests are the right thing, and as in so many cases already, will conclude that agricultural interests should not exist at all. Similarly, rather than sneaking into dog shows and releasing the dogs from the safe confines of their crates, all domestic animals will be returned to the wild.

The reality is, any and all domesticated animals who are placed in the setting of the wild, without human ownership, will not survive. Mother Nature is a predator and does not provide for those who are not also preying on others.

James Serpell, a professor at the University of Pennsylvania, has said: "The thing about mandatory spay-neuter is that those who are most willing to have their dogs spayed or neutered tend to be responsible people. And often, their dogs also happen to be nice animals in temperament. So what you're doing essentially is taking those dogs out of the breeding population. What will become of dog ownership if only the ill-tempered puppies from disreputable breeding programs are available?"

Dog and cat owners have understood and accepted the idea that responsible pet ownership involves being responsible regarding pet reproduction. The fact is, current breeding practices in most communities, in homes of most owners, is not the problem. Nationally, over 87 percent of dogs have already been surgically neutered. The problem is with those few who do not take responsibility for their pets, and allow them to roam, breed randomly and then walk away from the resulting progeny. Add to that the rise of imported animals, largely from our southern border by impoverished people who see a market for their new-found business interests, and yes, we have a problem.

The problem is all of our legislative efforts and energy is going toward those who are already responsible, by and large. The reason is simple: We are following a program proposed by those who are using animal welfare as a marketing mechanism, but whose real agenda is Animal Rights. They appear on TV with some unfortunate looking puppy or kitten and tell us for $19.00 a month we can end animal abuse. But the money they raise does not go to animal shelters or animal treatment; it goes for lavish salaries for executive staffs and paid lobbyists who propose animal rights legislation across the nation.

Let me share with you a recent conversation I had with a legislator. With the current economy in the tank and more problems looming on the horizon, I proposed the legislature pass a law stating that tomorrow there would be 250,000 new jobs in our state which would almost wipe out our record unemployment rate. He stuttered a minute and then replied they could not do that because it was illogical and would not do what it proposed to do. I agreed with him. The point was the passing of a law does not, in and of itself, create an economic flow of capital, nor does it create prosperity. He agreed. But I continued... So why then do legislators assume their addressing of problems with increasingly strict laws will make any difference?

He stuttered again and then responded, "But someone has to do something!" I laughed and asked simply, "Why?" And I ask the same question in regards to animal legislation. If it has no effect and does not address the real issue, why do we think by legislation and creating another ordinance and enforcement responsibility, we do anything to solve the problem.

First of all, I contend we have enough animal abuse laws already. If enforced, existing law would take care of the problems we face with pets on our streets. The problem is not that we do not have legal tools with which to attack the problem but that government budgets and practices do not have the resources and time to enforce them. If that is true to any degree, why then do we want to enact more laws and restrictions we will not be able to enforce? Ultimately, we create an environment in which we have satisfied our conscience that we have done our part to protect the unfortunate animals who are owned by evil owners and breeders, but all we have really done is create a new level of outlaws who, before the legislation, were responsible owners.

So, in the immortal words of Rodney King, "why can't we all just get along?" Good idea. Great idea! The problem is there is no arena of compromise. The process that exists between the legislators and the people being legislated against is one of finding a definition and wording of the ordinances. Following our last legislative season I was personally involved in a number of legislative planning sessions in which local breeders and interested parties were invited to give input into the wording and scope of the proposed legislation. When I proposed we did not need the legislation at all, and that it was proposed for the wrong purpose from sources with a wrong agenda, there were dead stares. So many breeders and animal sports people were involved in drafting the language of the legislation. No one would consider the question of not having the legislation at all.

Ultimately the legislation passed, after being review and altered at many levels, and the wording of the concerned breeders and sports enthusiasts was changed until it had no effect at all. The paid lobbyists won in closed meeting at other levels of the process, and we, the animal welfare contingent, had no say in the matter simply because we did not know how to do what the paid animal rights lobbyist did. It is a greater issue than the wording of a piece of legislation. The issue is the presence of the legislative sweep itself. It is a created phenomenon. It is created by organizations committed to a cultural philosophy which is not in the interest of animal ownership and enjoyment. It is created specifically to eliminate our rights and relationship to our domestic animals. It is a war, calculated and organized by our enemies, and we have not recognized that as yet. Neither have our local legislators.

Chapter Twelve

A Look at HSUS - The Humane Society of the United States

Wayne Pacelle (President of the Humane Society of the United States, former Executive Director of Fund for Animals)

"One generation and out. We have no problems with the extinction of domestic animals. They are creations of human selective breeding."

Though borrowing from a traditional use of the name "Humane" for local shelters and organizations, the HSUS has departed from that actual concept years ago.

HSUS is big, rich, and powerful - a "humane society" in name only. Most local animal shelters are under-funded and unsung, but the HSUS has accumulated $113 million in assets. It has built an international network of organizations by using the humane name for the emotions it evokes. The enormous budget HSUS raises every year could operate and sustain shelters in every state, but alas, none of it goes to local animal shelters at all.

In 2004 HSUS President Wayne Pacelle described some of his goals in *The Washington Post*: "We will see the end of wild animals in circus acts ... and we're phasing out animals used in research. Hunting? I think you will see a steady decline in numbers." In a June 2005 interview, Pacelle told *Satya* magazine that HSUS is working on "a guide to vegetarian eating, to really make the case for it." Pacelle, who is a strict vegan himself added, "Reducing meat consumption can be a tremendous benefit to animals."

After Pacelle joined HSUS in 1994, he told *Animal People* his goal was to build "a National Rifle Association of the animal rights movement." It is obvious now, as the organization's leader, he is, in fact backing up his rhetoric with the programs and focus that carries out those goals. In 2005 Pacelle announced the formation of the "Animal Protection Litigation Section" within HSUS, whose goal and operational philosophy is "the process of researching, preparing, and prosecuting animal protection lawsuits in state and federal court."

The Center for Consumer Freedom writes, "There is an enormous difference between animal "welfare" organizations, which work for the humane treatment of animals, and animal "rights" organizations, which aim to completely end the use and ownership of animals. The former have been around for centuries; the latter emerged in the 1980s, with the rise of the radical People for the Ethical Treatment of Animals (PETA)."

Shortly after his taking over the presidency of HSUS, Pacelle issued his agenda statement for the organization. HSUS's new "campaigns section," Pacelle wrote, "will focus on farm animals." Although the American culture is used to eating meat, eggs, and dairy foods, the concept of this animal rights organization with a budget three times the size of PETA's, aimed at their food choices should be unsettling. In fact, the thought of an organization so specifically focused on any choice we make in a free society should be unsettling.

Pacelle has hired an entire staff of high-profile, unapologetic meat and dairy "abolitionists" since he become president. In 2005, Compassion Over Killing (COK) President Miyun Park joined HSUS on staff in the "farm animals and sustainable agriculture department." Shortly thereafter, HSUS hired COK's other co-founder, Paul Shapiro, as manager of its derogatorily named "Factory Farming Campaign." Then COK's former general counsel Carter Dillard shortly afterward. All of these new staffers were, like Pacelle, self-described vegans. This gathering of vegan executives and staffers signaled the HSUS was establishing an anti-meat philosophy and setting itself to engage in campaigns against the agricultural community.

Robert Baker, an HSUS consultant and former chief investigator, told *U.S. News & World Report*: "The Humane Society should be worried about protecting animals from cruelty. It's not doing that. The place is all about power and money." HSUS employees have complained to the press that their organization wastes its resources on fundraising expenses and high salaries for its chief executives, and does little to actually provide hands on care of animals.

At the 1996 HSUS annual meeting, Wayne Pacelle announced legislative proposals and ballot initiatives would be used for all manner of legislation in the future, including "companion animal issues and laboratory animal issues." These operations, he said, "pay dividends and serve as a training ground for activists."

By hiding/ downplaying their radical associations and terrorist affiliations, the HSUS has gained a great deal of acceptance in our American mainstream culture. One of those questionable arenas of acceptance is into the American public school system. The National Association for Humane and Environmental Education, an arm of the HSUS, has developed a series of animal-rights-oriented publications. Through this means the HSUS spreads animal-rights propaganda to school children as young as five.

One of those publications, titled *People and Animals - A Humane Education Guide*, lists films and books as resources for teachers to use in the education of students. The suggested teaching aids label sport hunters as "selective exterminators" and "drunken slobs" who participate in a "blood sport" and a "war on wildlife" with "maniacal attitudes toward killing."

Conversely, HSUS criticizes curriculum materials in schools that tell about the use of animals in medical research: "These materials inappropriately target young people, who do not possess the cognitive ability to make meaningful decisions regarding highly controversial and complex issues." Obviously the concern is not for an even handed educational process for the students but for an advantage for HSUS propaganda.

Many Animal Rights organizations were surprised when the Humane Society of the United States in April 2000 sent John "J.P." Goodwin to China on an anti-fur trip. Goodwin was not just an animal activist - he was then an avowed member of the terrorist Animal Liberation Front (ALF). Following the trip he was hired by the HSUS as a legislative affairs staffer. Goodwin changed his manner of speech to be more consistent with the HSUS public image, and dropped his endorsement of violence.

"J. P." Goodwin is a high-school dropout who co-founded the Texas-based Coalition to Abolish the Fur Trade. His priorities were exposed when he said on a social email list, "My goal is the abolition of all animal agriculture." Goodwin has been arrested and convicted for his involvement as leader of a gang which vandalized fur retailers in many states in the 1990s. In 2000 an animal-rights newspaper *Animal People News* featured Goodwin, noting that he "gleefully announced a string of Animal Liberation Front mink releases and arsons against furriers and fur farms" while a "spokesman" for the underground terrorist group.

Goodwin held a press conference in Petaluma, California, about a slaughterhouse arson, and "shocked the public with his comments on the March 1997 arson at a farmer's feed co-op in Utah, referring to a fire that caused almost $1 million in damage and could easily have killed a family sleeping on the premises." Goodwin later told The Deseret News: "We're ecstatic."

Funds and Funny Transactions

IRS reports in 1998 and 1999, reveal the Humane Society of the United States made financial contributions to WASTE.org, an Internet website that was the main connection for the terrorist Animal Liberation Front (ALF).

Continued probes by the IRS show their concern about funds raised for animal welfare but used for the broader agenda of radical animal rights agendas through other organization of a more violent and radical nature. Possibly it is not a supporting of organizations of a different nature and agenda, but the revelation of what HSUS is really all about.

Chapter Thirteen

A Look at PETA - People for the Ethical Treatment of Animals

Ingrid Newkirk - National Director of PETA (People for the Ethical Treatment of Animals):

"For one thing we would no longer allow breeding. People could not create different breeds. If people had companion animals in their homes, these animals would have to be refugees from the animal shelter and the streets ... But as the surplus of cats and dogs declined, eventually companion animals would be phased out and we would return to a more symbiotic relationship - enjoyment at a distance."

Ingrid Newkirk again: "Pet ownership is an absolutely abysmal situation brought about by human manipulation."

If hypocrisy is the mother of all credibility problems, then People for the Ethical Treatment of Animals (PETA) have their hands full. While they attack restaurant owners, grocers, farmers, dog clubs, scientists, breeders, anglers, and countless other Americans, and complain about the "unethical" treatment of animals, the group has its own dirty little secret.

PETA kills animals by the thousands, year after year. From July 1998 through December 2009, People for the Ethical Treatment of Animals (PETA) killed over 23,000 dogs, cats, and other "companion animals." That's more than five defenseless creatures every day. PETA has a walk-in freezer to store the dead bodies, and contracts with a Virginia Beach company to cremate them.

Not counting the pets PETA spayed and neutered, the group put to death over 90 percent of the animals it took in during the last five years. While espousing a compassionate philosophy toward animals, their own euthanizing program seems to say otherwise. This agenda has been ignored. Maybe it *is* in keeping with some mysterious rationalization of the face value of PETA's statement of purpose.

In 2002 the PETA federal income-tax return claimed a $9,370 write-off for a giant walk-in freezer. While this kind of freezer might be used for meat storage or ice cream for most companies, animal-rights activists don't eat meat or dairy foods. During a 2007 criminal trial, a PETA manager (testifying under oath) confirmed the obvious -- that the group uses the appliance to store the bodies of dead animals it euthanizes. . .

In 2000, the Associated Press first noted PETA's Kervorkian-esque tendencies. PETA President Ingrid Newkirk complained that actually taking care of animals costs more than killing them: "We could become a no-kill shelter immediately," she admitted. It was evident the message and the practice of this organization were two different things. Possibly it really is about the money rather than the treatment of animals.

Does this mean PETA kills animals, simply because it has other financial priorities?

PETA receives almost $30 million each year in income, much of it raised from pet owners who believe their donations actually help animals. Instead, the group spends its budget and donations on programs equating people who eat chicken with Nazis, scaring young children away from drinking milk, recruiting children into the radical animal-rights lifestyle, and intimidating businessmen and their families in their own neighborhoods. PETA has also shelled out thousands of dollars for the defense of arsonists, animal terrorists and other violent extremists.

PETA proclaims it's outrageous media-seeking stunts are "for the animals." Yet, how about the animals turned in to their own shelter? Complaining about what the American people eat for dinner while administering lethal injections to puppies and kittens isn't ethical. It's hypocritical -- with a death toll that PETA would protest if it weren't their own.

People for the Ethical Treatment of Animals (PETA) is an avowed animal rights organization headquartered in Norfolk, Virginia, USA. It has two million members worldwide, and claims the status of the largest animal rights group in the world. (HSUS seems to be larger both in budget and influence, but then who's measuring?) Ingrid Newkirk, international president of PETA, said, "our goal is total animal liberation."

Founded in 1980 as a nonprofit, tax exempt, 501(c)(3) corporation, it is funded almost entirely by its members. PETA's website espouses four core issues: 1. factory farming, 2. fur farming, 3. animal testing, and 4. animals in entertainment. As to the ownership of pets it says: "We at PETA very much love the animal companions who share our homes, but we believe that it would have been in the animals' best interests if the institution of 'pet keeping' - i.e., breeding animals to be kept and regarded as 'pets'—never existed". Pet ownership is, it says, "selfish desire to possess animals and receive love from them." They do not claim directly to endorse "setting them free," although many of the animal rights extremist organizations that they freely associate with do. PETA campaigns against the abuse of backyard dogs, of course, as well as cock fighting, dog fighting and bullfighting.

But they also campaign against hunting, and fishing, and against killing animals regarded as pests... with the exception of those animals that are turned into their shelter. Their slogan is "animals are not ours to eat, wear, experiment on, or use for entertainment." The abbreviated version might be best said as, "Animals are not ours."

PETA's style has been blatantly confrontational and its campaigns at least controversial if not downright crude. It has been criticized for giving financial support to persons associated with the Earth Liberation Front and Animal Liberation Front, which were listed in a draft planning document as domestic terrorist threats by the U.S. Department of Homeland Security.

Newkirk is outspoken in her promotion of direct action even when it is illegal. PETA has provided financial support to militant activists, and PETA members and staff have themselves been criticized for taking too radical of action. In January 2010, a member of the Canadian parliament described the throwing of a pie at the Fisheries Minister by a PETA member as "acting as a terrorist organization." They have been involved in efforts to halt the fur industry, which has involved disrupting fashion shows and throwing red paint on the runway. In 1996, PETA activists famously threw a dead raccoon onto the restaurant table of Anna Wintour, the editor-in-chief of *Vogue*, who promotes the use of fur, and left bloody paw prints and the words "Fur Hag" on the steps of her home.

Newkirk has also cooperated with ALF raids. During Coronado's trial for an arson attack on Michigan State University in 1995, U.S. Attorney Michael Dettmer said Newkirk had arranged, "before the fact, to have Coronado send her documents from the lab and a videotape of the raid." Newkirk never made an apology for her support of activists who may break the law, writing that "no movement for social change has ever succeeded without 'the militarism component'." Speaking of the Animal Liberation Front, she says: "Thinkers may prepare revolutions, but bandits must carry them out."

In 2005 police discovered that over 80 animals had been euthanized and left in area dumpsters. Two PETA employees were seen putting the animal carcasses in a dumpster. They were driving a van registered to PETA and had left behind 18 dead animals; 13 more were inside the van. The animals had been euthanized by the PETA employees immediately after taking them from shelters in Northampton and Bertie counties. The employees said they were euthanizing animals in some rural contract North Carolina shelters after it found the shelters were killing animals in ways PETA considered inhumane. They were charged by police with 31 felony counts of animal cruelty and eight misdemeanor counts of illegal disposal of dead animals.

It is hard to take any of these extremist organizations seriously when their practice is so flexible. They do what they stand against/ what they have billed as the purpose of their organization. It is obvious that the structures of money, power and position are far more central to their purpose than their stated goals.

And yet, as inconsistent as they may be, the general public and legislators still look to them for expertise and input in the process of proposing legislation to stamp out the evils of those they target. This dichotomy of process and purpose leaves one wondering if the state's focus and legislative efforts might be best spent looking into the organizations who propose such nonsense in the first place. Maybe that legislative effort might be best used outlawing some of these organizations.

Chapter Fourteen

Animal Rights or Animal Welfare?

There are many other animal rights organization other than those mentioned here. They range from the sincere and ethical to the radical, terrorist, extremist. Although their methods differ, and the way they conduct business varies, they have a basic common philosophy: remove animals from being defined as private property, and elevate their status. Give animals rights equal that of human beings. This presents several problems:

1. How would they access those rights?

No one would argue that animals should be guaranteed humane and proper respect and treatment. Animal abuse is simply wrong - absolutely wrong. No argument. But if responsibility for animals is removed from owners and placed in the decision-making power of the state, then it is a question of how they would articulate their problem, justify their claim and present their case.

It is at this juncture we expose a major problem. The animal rights activists are declaring, by the very act of asking for animals to have 'human' rights, that they are speaking for the animals. The activists are prepared to carry an advocacy role into the courts on behalf of the animals. So in fact, we are bypassing the responsibility of the owner and substituting something else: an authority who does not live with the animal, understand the dynamics of the family where the animal lives and may have little or no experience with animals... We are appointing these activists to 'speak for the animals.' Does this sound asinine to anyone else? What it does is create a middle man between owner and animal, with the presumption that the "advocate" knows best/ actually knows more about the animal than the owner does. Not only is this cumbersome and awkward, it is presumptuous and just plain wrong.

We can only conclude "animal rights" is a system of ideological belief as rigid (and vulnerable to unreasoning abuse) as any religion. If abuse of animals in the general public is a problem, just wait until abuses of power are unleashed upon animals by those who "speak for them." I simply want to stand and shout, "speak for any animal you want to, but I will allow mine to speak for themselves." The ramification of this movement and its predictable end result is obvious, yet we as a culture are marching toward it headlong.

There is a simple solution. That is to limit governmental function involved with animal welfare. First of all, we cannot guarantee happiness to people let alone animals, so whether they are happy or not is beside the point. The issue is, are they cared for? Do they have adequate shelter, food, health care, exercise, and hygiene? It is proper for the state to protect the animals, children or anyone else from mistreatment by irresponsible humans, but it is not OK for the state to remove the responsibility that God gave to us for our personal property.

There is more to consider here than our current legal frame work. We have a legal history and frame of reference that is violated by this current wave of animal rights nonsense. The whole of the Judeo-Christian ethic, which evolved into common law upon which our legal system is based, presumes certain God-given, obvious, self-evident truths. It is on this basis that both the Declaration of Independence and the Constitution describes our human rights. They do not enumerate our animals' rights, for the presumption of the ethic and of history is that human kind was placed over animals for their care in the creative scope of things, and that animals are here for our oversight and use. That use includes work, play, love and yes, food.

To alter that presumption is to overturn thousands of years of the foundation and development of our law and ethics. It throws a presumption into the law that should not and cannot be tolerated. It asserts that human rights and animal relationships are to be determined by government, and they are not given by our Creator. This change of presumption is huge. It is more than a cultural shift from one form to another; it attempts to invoke the power of government in granting rights and position in human structures, implying government is superior to God Himself. It is a religious matter as well as a legal matter.

From this perspective it is easy to see why a person faith (Jewish faith, Christian faith or presumably the Muslim faith) could not support the concept of animal rights. It is simply unconscionable to throw away the responsibility of human kind regarding oversight of the animals given into our care. This rejection of history; this philosophical shift, goes to the roots of our religious underpinnings and demands the rejection of God. This is not easy for the culture who anciently chose the companionship and interrelationship with animals. But it is probably not difficult for those who can conceive of their own elitist capacity to speak for the animals, for this rising new culture has, in large part, rejected the existence of God already.

So the issue, basically and without complicated discussion of all ramifications, is whether our focus will be on animal welfare or animal rights. If it is to be animal welfare then the animal

93

rights folks will be offended and have to find another avenue for hawking their superiority to the rest of the human race. But if our governmental officials and staff move into the animal rights agenda, as they seem to be doing, it is going to require a philosophical and cultural shift from our agricultural roots that cannot happen easily. I have already decided. I cannot and will not change my religious structures and understanding of God and His creative organization, and I will not allow my animals to be victimized by organization of animal rights people or the government, regardless of how well-meaning they are. I will not give up my rights to my animals as private property.

Chapter Fifteen

What Does This Mean
for Our Society?

It is not just that we are facing a contrast in our view of animals, but that our entire culture is at risk at the moment. Our economic underpinnings are shifting and uncertain. Our diverse cultures are developing separately and we are on the verge of collapse unless something dynamic happens. Our government is underfunded and grasping for sources of revenue. We have pressures, tensions and trouble on every hand.

The options are to find a way to stabilize our culture where it is, collapse entirely, or make a giant step into the future. I would argue that it cannot be stabilized. The diversity of this nation culturally, and the development of separate, contrasting cultures cannot be changed. We will inevitably become enemies and degenerate into regional culture wars unless we can find some central way to move closer together in a united step into the future.

As our cultural differences determine economic differences, and our political differences widen and threaten to divide us even more, there has to be some liberating influence that will centralize us. We must focus, gather our energy, and stave off a fragmented future. If the growth of governmental restriction and problem-solving by legislation continue, frustrations will simply garner rejection and ultimately rebellion. If that course is not altered, we are headed for a revolution and the breaking down of our national boundaries into regional nations underpinned by some common and central philosophies of life.

The issues of animal control are not central to all of this; they are simply symptoms of a greater cultural and philosophical battle. They do, however, play a key role in defining how we are going to negotiate this press by the new world order of things. Our traditional approach to animals and their relationship with us is one of the many things at stake. HSUS, PETA and all the other new organizations in our nation will prevail, and we will have no animals, no rights and no financial opportunities. Or we will define our objections to their beliefs and reject them. But will we have a lot of meaningless and ineffective laws "stopping crime, creating jobs," and other well-meaning attempts to deal with human problems, but no nation to govern?

This is a time to consider the prospects of great change. It is a time to decide what direction we want to go. It is a time to shore up our philosophical underpinnings and beliefs and to determine whether or not we are ready to stand on them or give them up. That includes our pets. If we are ready to give them up I suspect the chaos they will experience will be nothing in comparison to our own.

Our world will change. It cannot be stopped. It is changing already as it has always been changing. But we are at a pivotal point of choosing the way we will move into the future. We will do so by actively joining those who presume they know best, how we should live and relate to our animals (or allowing an unconscious shift in that direction). Or we fight for our current government – a stable rule of law – and move on to the next age with a greater sense of what freedom is and how we can enjoy it, without the shadow of more regulations or organizations of superiority undermining those freedoms. There is nothing better than our freedom, and we should permit nothing to take it away.

Chapter Sixteen

Declining Supply

While 147 pieces of legislation were proposed in 37 states last year, more than 33 states passed regulations targeting animal breeders. While the target was stated to be puppy mills, the end result was that almost every hobby breeder in the nation is place in a position where they can continue their passion illegally or quit altogether.

Patti Strand, executive director of the National Animal Interest Alliance (NAIA), an animal-welfare organization aligned with purebred breeders and pet enthusiasts, states that this country is truly at a turning point.

American Kennel Club (AKC) registrations have posted sharp decreases since 1992 levels, and the numbers for all purebred animals are thought to be on the decline as well. What is up, however, are purebred dog imports. Not only have we as a nation, legislated American industry to the point that we are no longer an industrial nation, relying on foreign nations for our production, we have now done it to our agricultural world, and even our pet production. The problem is, just as we have faced recalls for lead in toys, poison in gluten products and a lack of quality control in general, foreign bred pet animals do not have the exacting standards of the American Kennel Club, its member breed clubs or its professional hobby breeders.

The end result is already disastrous to our domestic animal registries and the impact has not yet been fully felt. This is not just a crisis time for the existence of the pure bred dog, it is an outright war between a traditional culture, who enjoy their animals, attend their competitions and the state and local governments of our nation who, through ignorance of this culture are cooperating in an all out assault by anti-animal forces.

Last year, NAIA tracked 700 pieces of legislation influencing its members. An evaluation of data from the AKC depicts registrations last year at 716,195 animals. Only half of purebred owners are believed to register their dogs through AKC. The data suggests last year's registrations are closer to 1965 levels, and Ms. Strand believes it will continue to spiral downward.

Take a look at the Dalmatian breed. Following a spike in breeding after the Disney release of *101 Dalmatians* in 1996, breed numbers have been plummeting. Breed registrations peaked in 1993 at 42,816 dogs and dropped to just 983 in 2008.

"Breeders have been the recipients of 30 years of really bad publicity during which time they have been portrayed as responsible for pet overpopulation, the creation of genetic diseases and bad temperaments," Strand says. "People come away thinking they just don't care about dogs."

While such organizations as The AKC Health Foundation, The German Shepherd Health Foundation, The Orthopedic Foundation for Animals and a host of other breed specific funding sources, search for the causes of diseases and the genetic structures of hereditary disease, the import animals and dogs bred randomly in the streets have no resources for the betterment of the reproductive lines or the future of our pet population.

Targeting the evils of puppy mills has become a byline for targeting all breeders who are characterized as brutish beasts who create the overpopulation of dogs and cats without conscience or concern. And they do it, we are told, for the

99

money, which any hobby breeder will tell you is an illusion of monumental proportions.

This all betrays the unethical practices of legislative members who, because of the limits of time and resources, do not investigate thoroughly the subject of their legislation, leaving it to the targeted outlaws to pay to go to court and reverse the legislation if they can. While the image of the unscrupulous breeder has grown to Steven King proportions, the reality is quite different. Here is a culture, accepted and revered in the past, who is attempting to survive quietly in the joys of animal sports, but has instead become the evil and corrupt monster of a new cultural setting.

"Very often the brush stroke is very broad, and it defines all breeders as part of the problem. It stigmatizes those who breed responsibly," Strand adds. And yet, legislative focus remains on stopping abuse by stopping animal production. We, the breeders of the country have not yet been able to communicate that animal welfare is different from animal rights and we are in favor of the enforcement of animal abuse laws and we are not in favor of the random breeding of animals by those who do not take responsibility for their dogs.

We also understand if we, as a society, continue to pursue our current course of action, we will end up with the few remaining breeders of the animal culture, safely behind bars while the random breeding continues and the imports fill our veterinary offices.

A 2008 American Pet Products Association study confirms this country is actively trying to spay and neuter its way out of a surplus of unwanted pets. In fact, the association estimates that 76 percent to 87 percent of pets were neutered in 2008, Strand says.

The question remains, when all of the pets are neutered, where will the supply come from for the next generation of pets? The answer is, they will not come from reputable breeders committed to reputable registries. Those people will all be in jail or out of business.

Chapter Seventeen

Social Egocentricity

There is this story about the blond who... OK! No one wants to hear another blond joke simply because they are so stereotypically not true. That does not mean that all blonds are smart or that all humans, regardless of their hair color, are smart. The human race comes in all sizes, colors, hair color genes, shapes and intelligence levels. There are people like Einstein and Hawkins and others, who are able to mentally probe the mysteries of the universe and come away with an explanation and plausible theory of grand and glorious things. There are also people on the other end of the spectrum who can't seem to make change for you when you buy a soft drink.

This gap in intelligence is nothing new. It is as old as humanity itself. We are simply different and the genetic gods do not play fair or distribute the intellectual wealth evenly. Life is not fair. Genetics is not fair. Intellectual equality is never going to happen.

Yet, there are those among us who presume they have the responsibility to right that inequity. They, presume to understand enough about themselves to know they have the intelligence and ability to make decisions for those who do not understand as well as they do. These are the egocentrics among us who presume that their role in life is to stand at the center of the universe and make sure everything rotates around them in an even and fair orbit. They are the social elite who tend to gravitate to positions of public power with the motivation to fix everything.

Narcissus, in Greek mythology, was the god who saw his reflection in the pool and fell in love with himself. As certainly as there are a variety of intellects, hair colors and personality types, the narcissistic live among us.

There was a funny young man in my college classes years ago who had a string of sayings about pride that were hilarious. He would occasionally tell someone about the book he had written entitled, "Humility and How I Attained It!" Then he would add, "I'm so proud that I am humble." But all the jokes aside, there are those who presume to be smarter than the rest of us. Well, let's face it, there are people smarter than most of us. That is not the problem. The problem comes when those who presume to be so, decide they should make the decisions for the rest of us because they know best.

The ethical question that arises here is, if people do make poor decisions, for their own sake, shouldn't someone who knows better make their decisions? If we answer yes, then we have betrayed a world view that espouses a politic and philosophy of social elitism. If I am smarter, then I am responsible to make the decisions. While that might be true in a corporate setting or a military setting where advancement in the chain of command makes on more responsible, it is not the philosophical foundation of our political culture. We are a nation founded on the premise that all men are created equal. OK, there is a problem with that observation if we expect equality to be general and even. If we suppose that the meaning of that phrase has to do with intellect, size, shape and or genetic balance, then we are going to be sadly disappointed with either the creation or the creator.

The equality spoken of is not dealing with a fair distribution of human resources but with the innate value of every person regardless of their difference. Every person is equal in the rights accorded to them by their creator. Whether they can handle them evenly or fairly is not at issue. The guarantee of the human right to life, liberty and the pursuit of happiness has nothing to do with an equal station in life but with the right to live it without the imposition of the elitism of superior people determining how I should live it.

Freedom does not guarantee there will be no bad decisions or no ignorant judgment. Freedom allows for error and recognizes evil. It has no utopian illusions but guarantees we can each express our own unique genius or make our own mistakes. It is the foundation for the free enterprise system of economics and the foundation stone for our political system that limits government control. The expectation of a free society is that the best and the brightest can enhance their lives and can even offer advice to we who are of diminished capacity, but they cannot rule us.

That whole foundational concept has been eroded in our current culture. It is somehow assumed the 'experts' among us have the right to decide what we should eat, what we should own, what our activities should be and how many marbles we should possess. They presume they should make sure their ideas and cultural values are presented to the legislature and enacted into law so that we, the people, do not make mistakes. How wonderful it is, they presume, for everyone to march in lockstep without error or deviation from the utopian plan they have devised.

This social elitism, or social geocentricism is catching and it is frankly, the most dangerous single enemy to our way of life. It is a wonderful thing for those who have the skill and intellect to be the deciders. It is also wonderful for those who follow their dictates and give up their mistake prone souls. It is a sickness that will ultimately kill our culture as it is trying daily to put to death the subcultures of our present world.

In this rush to regulate humanity, law and behavior, we buy into the presumption of superiority at one extreme and incompetence on the other. The fact is, people do make mistakes, including the intelligent elite. But the philosophical perspective that those who do make mistakes should be limited so they do not is contrary to every freedom we know. It is not the responsibility of government to find ways to limit human failure but to remain within its own limited scope of authority and to allow for human failure. For once we design the standardization for human non-failure we permit government to go beyond its prescribed limits and we limit the genius of humanity. That's right - the genius of humanity is revealed in the freedom of the individual to be wrong and to deviate from the norm and to express their creativity. There is genius in the average man. That genius will be corrected by peer pressure and by the market place. Whether it is genius or not can only be determined by trial and error and by its exposure to the market place. When government takes the role of deciding what is and what is not worthy of the market place, we have stopped progress and made a mockery of the freedoms prescribed in our founding documents.

Chapter Eighteen

The Problem with Breeders

The current animal culture war is complex and difficult for the non-animal person to understand. While the multimillion dollar animal rights corporations sent their paid lobbyists across the nation proposing anti-animal legislation, the average pet person does not even know there is trouble brewing. They hear the commercials from the animal rights people and, since they always include a cute puppy or kitten who is presumably abused, they tend to emotionally accept the rhetoric of the commercial. The wording is being changed, from a 'pet' who has an 'owner' to a 'companion' animal. The underlying reason for the shift in terms is determined by the philosophical agenda - to change the status of the animal from owned personal property to being an equal to its human companion and thus having human like rights.

Of course, no true animal lover is in favor of animal abuse, but while that appears to be the issue, it could not be further from the truth. What has happened is the large well funded animal rights organizations have seemingly successfully turned the average animal lover against other animal lovers, the breeders of the dogs and cats they love. Let's look for a minute at the profile of those who are involved in this war:

1. The average American family with their pet.

This category loves their pet, hates to think of animals being abused and is one of the funding sources ('saving a pet at $19.00 a Month') for the animal rights groups.

2. The show exhibitor and enthusiast and hobby breeder.

This category loves their pets, makes them more central to their lives as they train, show and breed for their future animals and for other enthusiasts and pet owners. These are also a category targeted by the animal rights agenda and characterized as the veil breeders.

3. The commercial breeders who breed and sell for the profits involved.

This category may also own pets and love them but their primary motivation in breeding is profit. They breed and sell with less scrutiny then the hobby breeder and with less responsibility for their 'product.' They see a market and breed to meet that market demand.

4. The backyard breeder.

These people are sincere, want to breed to show the kids how birth occurs, or want to make sure fluffy experiences having puppies once in her life, or think of themselves as hobby breeders but who simply do not know what they are doing. They do not do health histories, do not know the value of a pedigree in predictive genetics and end up with a litter without any market or relationship to an established sport, club or demand for their animals.

5. The random breeding mill.

This category produces far more animals than all the others put together. These are the people who are irresponsible, have a pet but do not take care of it, allow it to run the streets and breed at random. The puppies and kittens from this category are unwanted, unplanned, have a low quality of care and a health history for the breeding is totally absent.

Category 1, the pet owner, is not a problem. They probably have spayed or neutered their pet and take care of it. Their lives revolve around their jobs, their children's activities and school, their weekend camping trip and other community interests. Seldom does their animal end up in a shelter.

Category 2, the show enthusiast and hobby breeder is also not the problem. They love their animals, some think too much, take them to field trials, agility competitions, obedience shows and conformation shows and more. They occasionally breed with the objective of bettering the breed, and only after doing the studies necessary to predict the genetic outcome of the litter. They have a reputation in their world which attracts their market and their breed club requires them to be responsible for their puppies for their entire lives. Few of this categories animals end up in a shelter. As a personal testimony, we have tried to stay in touch with our puppies throughout their entire lives and in over 55 years of breeding, to our knowledge, we have never had one of our dogs go to a shelter. We have taken several back over those years and kept them to live out their lives with us. By and large, this category does not contribute to the population of animal shelters, but is the target of the animal rights agenda and much of the animal legislation craze that is happening today.

Category 3, the commercial breeders are considered a major problem by the animal rights corporations. TV news magazines have featured this category, demonizing them as the major problem in the animal world. But they are regulated by the U. S. D. A. which requires regular inspections and health certificates. These breeders sell their product through pet stores, on the internet and in ads in national dog magazines and newspapers. They are market driven, producing what they calculate will fill the demand of the pet market and usually have experience in doing so. Their usual product is a pure bred dog with registration papers, but without a health history or guarantee other than the animal is healthy when sold.

This category is characterized as the puppy mill with terrible conditions and abused puppies. Although there certainly are cases where this has been true, as in all things, it is unfair to characterize all breeding businesses by the evils of a few. It is also difficult to establish this source of supply is directly responsible for the overpopulation of animals in our shelters. We might argue the indiscriminate sales of these animals without personal contact with the customer and customer screening is a problem, but the direct relationship between the purchaser and the animal they purchase is the real issue. Some people simply should not buy an animal. The problem is in administering that issue. If government does it, then it is an imposition to our personal freedoms, but if I as a breeder do it, it is my right to screen my customers and to follow-up to see that the dog has a forever home. Although this category of breeder may indirectly affect the market, it would be difficult to determine that they are, simply by their existence, evil. Yet, legislation and animal rights activities focus directly at them.

Category 4, the backyard breeder, is seldom a focus of the animal rights corporations or legislation. Although increasingly legislation is requiring spay and neuter of all pets, many of those who would fit into this category are ignorant of the provisions and choose to breed anyway. When the animals do not sell, or their lack of health planning shows up with a problem litter, these are a major source of animals dumped on the local shelter. And the backyard breeder does not take responsibility for the long term welfare of the animal. They in fact probably have not thought through the possibility they will end up with returned animals, sick animals or the expense of treatment for sick or deformed animals. They just did not know.

By the use of the term, backyard breeder, we are not referring to the location of the breeding, for most hobby breeders breed and raise their puppies in their homes, but the term is in reference to a general lack of knowledge and professional skills that predisposes the animals produced to less than ideal situations. These animals may be registered pure bred animals but more than likely will be un-papered, supposedly pure bred or some mixture with genetic backgrounds that even God cannot keep up with.

Category 5, the random breeding mill is by far the least likely to have any responsibility toward their litter, or litters as the case may be, and may not even go as far as dropping them at the local shelter, allowing them to find homes on their own or in many cases, becoming wild animals in roving packs, living off of the land. This category is seldom targeted by animal rights groups or legislation for there is no opportunity for enforcement and no way to get their attention.

Clearing the Air

Let me speak clearly here. I am under attack for enjoying the heritage passed down by my parents of loving animals. I am part of a subculture of pure bred dog enthusiasts who raise a few dogs, enjoy the competition with other enthusiasts of our dogs in healthy loving dog shows and exhibitions. I do not contribute to the overpopulation of unwanted dogs in shelters or running our streets, and my dogs love to be pampered as they are and to live in the comfortable confines of their home. Our relationship is one founded in love and sustained in a continued commitment to the betterment of the breed.

I will not accept the argument that we and those who enjoy this cultural life style with us, are ruining the world and contributing to the overpopulation of animals and to the cruelty and abuse of the animal rights commercials, formatted to raise even more money. I will not accept the supposed millions of unwanted animals euthanized each year is my fault.

When I was a vegetable-hating child, my mother used to argue at dinner time the starving children in China would benefit from my eating my vegetables. I never did get a thank you card from China after eating those terrible things and rejected the logic even while eating them. So, I am not predisposed now to accept the logic that my responsible love of my animals and my animal sports are causing other people to be irresponsible. And, I will not accept the legislators' logic that says spaying and neutering my show dogs, which will automatically make them ineligible to show, will shut down the shelters for lack of business. If the target is wrong then we are shooting the wrong people.

I further contend that my love for my breed is not evil either. I fell in love with my first German Shepherd Dog in 1954 and have been in love with them ever since. While they are increasingly being included in breed specific legislation, I am increasingly wondering why and agitated at the ignorance of it all.

My breed has been used for police work, rescue work, search and rescue, military work, drug sniffing, bomb sniffing, cancer sniffing, and more than 100 specific uses in working to benefit humanity. So if communities across America determine this is an aggressive and dangerous breed and should be eliminated from the canine gene pool, the next time your child is missing or your community has a natural disaster and needs search and rescue or your police force needs a good dog, call for the local Mutt owners. But if humanity benefits from my breed, then let's honor them for the work they do and the place they hold in human service.

I also contend the pure bred dog is not the problem. I fail to see how my choice of a pure bred dog causes the euthanizing of a shelter dog. I did not breed the shelter dog nor did I abandon it to the shelter. How about yelling at the idiots who irresponsibly bred those dogs, I did not do it. And if you per chance sometime in the future should find one of my dogs in the shelter, call me. I will be there in fifteen minutes to pick it up. I'll deal with the person I sold it to later, without legislation, face to face. I will not accept guilt without responsibility. It is illogical and it is dangerous.

The legislative logic for this problem is also flawed. It is like hunting for a dangerous bear, but finding none, shooting the neighbor's sheep instead. If you can't legislate effectively against those who are the real problem, why legislate against those who are not the problem? It seems legislation must be passed to keep the office holder's job intact. So legislation happens whether or not it is needed. The problem is *where* it will go, not *whether* it will. The whole logic of the need to legislate everything escapes me.

Defining Our Terms

I own my animals. While I love them and care for them better than most people do their children, they do not have opposing thumbs and are not mentally capable of taking care of themselves. Why animal rights extremists will argue that we took the wolf out of the wild and domesticated it and that Mother Nature wants them back in the wild, the fact is the domesticated animals are not suited to the wild. And again, I will not allow a wild eyed animal terrorist to make me feel guilty for perpetuating the station of my animals. I like it the way it is and

112

so do my dogs. Besides, Mother Nature is not a kind lady. She is a harsh taskmaster and serial killer. Wild animals do not have it so good and domesticated animals in the wild are simply meals on wheels.

So the ownership of animals is a traditional concept and elevating them to have their own rights in a legal sense does them no good and complicates the whole issue of animal welfare. If they are our personal property then we are responsible for their care. If the animal rights agenda wins out and destroys our culture, then no one is responsible except the elite organizations who propose this madness. God help us if our animals are ever released from the personal responsibility of their masters. Again, the issue is animal welfare, not animal rights.

The demand across the nation to communities and legislative bodies is to change the language from 'owner' to 'guardian' in the human/pet relationship. While the significance escapes the average person and pet owner, the change signifies a change of legal status and is an attempt to remove the pet from the protection of being personal property. Courts in various parts of the country have recently affirmed the traditional concept of the pet as personal property and thus not subject to confiscation by officers of the law without due process. Yet, the attempt to reclassify the pet continues with the ignorant cooperation of the public and legislators.

Chapter Nineteen

Utopia in an Imperfect World

In quantum mechanics, the Heisenberg uncertainty principle states that certain pairs of physical properties, like position and momentum, cannot both be known to arbitrary precision. That is, the more precisely one property is known, the less precisely the other can be known.

While uncertainty and imperfection are constants in our world there remains those who propose that this state of imperfection, in and of itself is somehow evil. There are those who, for whatever reason, dedicate their lives to eradicating the imperfections around them, and more often than not, end up frustrated and lonely as the imperfections and uncertainties continue with hardly a notice of their heroic efforts.

Those who breed dogs and enjoy the world of animal interaction are seldom caught by the illusion that perfection is possible. Their efforts to breed the perfect dog, or whatever animal they are involved with, is all too often far short of the goal. While there is a perfect standard in each breed, the reality is never exactly what the standard describes. And, as much as we study the results of genetics and form genetic theories, imperfection happens. Occasionally we get really close and assume that we are almost there and then Heisenberg whispers his uncertainty principle into our ear and we relax to enjoy the resulting progeny of those we felt good enough to carry on our line. Life is uncertain. Our world is imperfect.

The science of physics has accepted that, while the general scheme of the universe is fundamentally precise, we are not, or at least are incapable of understanding all of the intervening dynamics of the universe. Yet we continue to study, experiment and to broaden our understanding. So also the hobby breeder, whose knowledge increases with each generation of breeding but whose awe of genetics broadens also with each discovery of the unexpected. Life really is uncertain. Our world really is imperfect.

At the center of the mortgage meltdown that recently prompted the crisis, were those theoretical constructs known as financial models. These models calculated the history of mortgages within the industry in an attempt to determine the degree of risk and values of the properties held in trust. The problem was they failed to predict. The models were imperfect. While some outside of the industry saw clouds on the horizon, those with the models were caught by surprise.

What went wrong? The modelers, as experienced and precise as they were, were caught by a fantasy of perfection that did not exist. There was an invisible virus working in the model that exposed a dark love of theoretical elegance and excessive precision.

The Utopian attempt to force the ugly stepsister's foot into Cinderella's pretty glass slipper did not work. It will never work for people are different and, yes, life is uncertain and our world is imperfect.

The Founding Fathers of this nation understood all of that when they set out to create a new nation. Their desire was not just to create another nation, but a 'NEW' nation. One that was established on new concepts of government, and that would not become just another nation like all the rest of the past. This new nation would not gain its human rights from the government but the government would not be allowed to prescribe rights. They would be 'recognized' rather than granted. They would be ascribed to the Creator God who gave them and government would be limited and not allowed to restrict those freedoms.

They understood the concepts of a world of uncertainty and a human race that was imperfect. In limiting government from the Utopian errors of the past, they set about to allow for that uncertainty and the imperfection of humanity. They understood that within that freedom great progress and advancement could be made, and yes, mistakes would be made. But the main focus of the Declaration of Independence and the forming of the Constitution was the limits of government and the freedom of the people, as imperfect as they may be. The model for our national government was unlike anything else in history in that it did not promise a Utopia nor expect perfect order or human perfection. The model was open ended, imprecise and non-confining. It did not require conformity to a given model of perfection, preferring to propose certain general criminal statutes and leaving vast areas of human activity to the individual.

In its resulting America the Beautiful, is the verification of the wisdom of our foundations where simplicity and variety gives way to the joy of accomplishment and the fulfillment of the desire for our personal property, real, animal or other.

Financial markets are alive. A financial model, however beautiful, is an artifice. To confuse the model with the world is to embrace a future disaster in the belief humans obey mathematical principles without any degree of uncertainty and without expressing imperfection.

How can we get our fellow modelers to give up their fantasy of perfection? We propose, not entirely in jest, a model makers'

Hippocratic Oath: Back off and do no harm! Or possibly we could also say, 'Take care of your own responsibilities and allow others to be responsible for themselves. You should not try to save the world.'

Yet, we have a world filled with those who would save us from ourselves, create a Utopian world to their model and decide for us under the assumption that we are incapable of deciding for ourselves. Such is the case in the advent of the animal rights movement, who have decided on a universal principle of animal rights and is hell bent in determination to sell it to everyone. Unfortunately they have found the willing mind of legislators across the land who similarly have gravitated to the halls of law making, which in and of itself may be like honey to the bears, an irresistible place to create a Utopian culture where human behavior and interest is prescribed down to the width of a dog hair. The error here is not that those who inhabit the legislative halls are evil, but that they are good, searching for ways to make our world more perfect, rather than doing as our Founding Fathers envisioned and leave the people to live their own lives.

"Conformity is the jailer of freedom and the enemy of growth." John F. Kennedy

Law has to do with conformity. It prescribes behavioral norms and determines between alternative values and actions. It brings our behavior in line with what is normal, as determined by the makers of the law. In the case of "Thou shalt not kill" it is good that we recognize murder is beyond the bounds of freedom and "your freedom ends where my nose begins." Absolute freedom from any restraints would probably be fine for the majority of people, but for those few who do not have a developed sense of responsibility and social grace, it is disastrous. But conversely, the proliferation of law can be so imposing as to incrementally squeeze us all into a rigid conformity that squeezes out any creativity, genius or freedom.

I am not arguing for anarchy but for a reversal of the current rush to solve all problems, or perceived problems with a law. The problem is, where there is any group who propose a law to regulate humanity to suit their desires, the effect is to choose one position or belief or activity over another. It would seem a far better solution to say:

- If you do not want to eat beef, stay out of McDonalds.
- If you are allergic to flowers stay away from the floral shop.
- If you do not like dogs, stay away from the dog shows.
- If...

The point is, there are many cultural groups in our world and in terms of solutions that exist between them, passing a law against one in favor of the other is hardly a solution at all. The animal rights activists have decided they do not like the animal world and want to regulate it and control it to suit their agenda. The solution is simple: Go away and stay away! We do not want your approval, your presence or your laws. We have been doing just fine for thousands of years before you existed. So go away!

The more we attempt to bring conformity the more we restrict creativity, genius and freedom. This is a universal principle. Law does not solve all problems, in fact, not all problems actually exist and need a solution. Sometimes the best action is no action at all.

Chapter Twenty

A Philosophical Issue

Unless law expresses a coherent philosophy and ethic, it fails to serve humankind. With the proliferation of law, from the federal arena through the state level and on to the local city and county, we have arrived at a time when those who make and administer the law are not philosophers at all, and thus, in so many cases, do not have a personal foundation to understand why and how they should make and administer the law.

It is this disparity of understanding and of commitment to some position that governs all we do, that is the greatest danger to our liberty. To build on the great body of documents produced by our Founding Fathers, without their philosophical understanding and purpose is to conflict or even destroy the nation they birthed. Today, we are in danger of this very thing.

The issue of Animal Rights and the contrasting concept of Animal Welfare each have philosophical underpinnings. They are not the same thing and unless we can conceive of which course we are following, we shall arrive nowhere. It is essential that the legislator, the enforcement arm of government and the judge understand and acknowledge which course they are following and what the outcome will be. This is not a matter of random passing of laws that feel good or that make the legislator look good. It is a conflicting course of belief one must decide upon.

For the sake of understanding, what follows is a presentation of various philosophers who have influenced our thought and

119

law to this point in history. It is simply excerpts from various works and is certainly not exhaustive or complete. It is hoped that it can, in general, serve to describe the different thought process and conclusions in this conflicting war or belief.

Descartes

His mechanistic approach was extended to the issue of animal <u>consciousness</u>. <u>Mind</u>, for Descartes, was a thing apart from the physical universe, a <u>separate substance</u>, linking human beings to the mind of God. The non-human, on the other hand, are nothing but complex <u>automata</u>, with no souls, minds, or reason. They can see, hear, and touch, but they are not, in any sense, conscious, and are unable to <u>suffer</u> or even to feel <u>pain</u>.

1693: Locke

John Locke argued against animal cruelty, but only because of the effect it has on human beings.

Against Descartes, the British philosopher John Locke (1632–1704) argued, in *Some Thoughts Concerning Education* in 1693, that animals do have feelings, and unnecessary cruelty toward them is morally wrong, but—echoing Thomas Aquinas—the right not to be so harmed adhered either to the animal's owner, or to the person who was being harmed by being cruel, not to the animal itself. Discussing the importance of preventing children from tormenting animals, he wrote: "For the custom of tormenting and killing of beasts will, by degrees, harden their minds even towards men."

1789: Bentham

Is it the faculty of reason or perhaps the faculty of discourse? But a full-grown horse or dog, is beyond comparison a more

120

rational, as well as a more conversable animal, than an infant of a day or a week or even a month, old. But suppose the case were otherwise, what would it avail? The question is not, Can they *reason*?, nor Can they *talk*? but, Can they *suffer?*

1824: Development of the concept of animal rights

The period saw the first extended interest in the idea that non-humans might have natural rights, or ought to have legal ones. In 1824, Lewis Gompertz, one of the men who attended the first meeting of the SPCA in June that year, published *Moral Inquiries on the Situation of Man and of Brutes*, in which he argued that every living creature, human and non-human, has more right to the use of its own body than anyone else has to use it, and our duty to promote happiness applies equally to all beings.

In 1879, Edward Nicholson argued in *Rights of an Animal* that animals have the same natural right to life and liberty that human beings do, arguing strongly against Descartes' mechanistic view, or what he called the "Neo-Cartesian snake," that they lack consciousness. Other writers of the time who explored whether animals might have natural rights were John Lewis, Edward Evans, and J. Howard Moore.

Late 1890s: Opposition to anthropomorphism

Richard Ryder writes that attitudes toward animals began to harden in the late 1890s, when scientists embraced the idea that what they saw as anthropomorphism—the attribution of human qualities to non-humans—was unscientific. Animals had to be approached as physiological entities only, as Ivan Pavlov wrote in 1927, "without any need to resort to fantastic speculations as

121

to the existence of any possible subjective states." This stance hearkened back to the position of Descartes in the 17th century that non-humans were purely mechanical, like clocks, with no rationality and perhaps even with no consciousness.

1975: Publication of *Animal Liberation*

Peter Singer's *Animal Liberation*, published in 1975, became pivotal. It was in a review of *Animals, Men and Morals* for the *New York Review of Books* on April 5, 1973, that the Australian philosopher, Peter Singer, first put forward his arguments in favor of animal liberation, which have become pivotal within the movement.[74] He based his arguments on the principle of utilitarianism, the view, broadly speaking, that an act is right insofar as it leads to the "greatest happiness of the greatest number," a phrase first used in 1776 by Jeremy Bentham in *A Fragment on Government*. He drew an explicit comparison between the liberation of women and the liberation of animals.

In 1970, over lunch in Oxford with fellow student Richard Keshen, who was a vegetarian, Singer first came to believe, by eating animals, he was engaging in the oppression of other species by his own. Keshen introduced Singer to the Godlovitches, and Singer and Roslind Godlovitch spent hours together refining their views. Singer's review of the Godlovitches' book evolved into *Animal Liberation*, published in 1975, now widely regarded as the "bible" of the modern animal rights movement.

1976: Founding of the Animal Liberation Front

Main articles: Animal Liberation Front, Timeline of ALF actions, Anarchism and animal rights, and Veganarchism

In parallel with the development of the Oxford Group, grassroots activists set up the Animal Liberation Front in 1976.

In parallel with the Oxford Group, grassroots activists were also developing ideas about animal rights. A British law student, Ronnie Lee, formed an anti-hunting activist group in Luton in 1971, later calling it the Band of Mercy after a 19th-century RSPCA youth group. The Band attacked hunters' vehicles by slashing tires and breaking windows, calling their brand of activism "active compassion." In November 1973, they engaged in their first act of arson when they set fire to a Hoechst Pharmaceuticals research laboratory near Milton Keynes. The Band claimed responsibility, identifying itself to the press as a "nonviolent guerilla organization dedicated to the liberation of animals from all forms of cruelty and persecution at the hands of mankind."

In August 1974, Lee and another activist were sentenced to three years in prison. They were paroled after 12 months, with Lee emerging more militant than ever. In 1976, he brought together the remaining Band of Mercy activists, with some fresh faces, 30 activists in all, in order to start a new movement. He called it the Animal Liberation Front (ALF), a name he hoped would come to "haunt" those who used animals.[80][82]

The ALF is now active in 38 countries, operating as a leaderless resistance, with covert cells acting on a need to know basis, often learning of each other's existence only when acts of "liberation" are claimed. Activists see themselves as a modern Underground Railroad, the network that helped slaves escape from the U.S. to Canada, passing animals from ALF cells, who have removed them from farms and laboratories, to sympathetic veterinarians to safe houses and finally to sanctuaries. Controversially, some activists also engage in sabotage and arson, as well as threats and intimidation, acts that have lost the movement a great deal of sympathy in mainstream public opinion.

The decentralized model of activism is intensely frustrating for law enforcement organizations, who find the cells and networks difficult to infiltrate, because they tend to be organized around known friends. In 2005, the U.S. Department of Homeland Security indicated how seriously it takes the ALF when it included them in a list of domestic terrorist threats.

The tactics of some of the more determined ALF activists are anathema to many animal rights advocates, such as Singer, who regard the animal rights movement as something that should occupy the moral high ground, an impossible claim to sustain when others are bombing buildings and risking lives in the name of the same idea. ALF activists respond to the criticism with the argument that, as Ingrid Newkirk of PETA puts it, "Thinkers may prepare revolutions, but bandits must carry them out."

Gary Francione: Abolitionism

Gary Francione: animals need only one right, the right not to be owned.

Abolitionism falls within the framework of the rights-based approach, though it regards only one right as necessary: the right not to be owned. Abolitionists argue the key to reducing animal suffering is to recognize legal ownership of sentient beings is unjust and must be abolished. The most prominent of the abolitionists is Gary Francione, professor of law and philosophy at Rutgers School of Law-Newark. He argues that focusing on animal welfare may actually worsen the position of animals, because it entrenches the view of them as property, and makes the public more comfortable about using them.

124

Francione calls animal rights group who pursue animal welfare issues, such as People for the Ethical Treatment of Animals, the "new welfarists," arguing that they have more in common with 19th-century animal protectionists than with the animal rights movement. He argues that there is no animal rights movement in the United States.

Carl Cohen

Carl Cohen argues that animals cannot distinguish their interests from what is right.

Critics such as Carl Cohen, professor of philosophy at the University of Michigan and the University of Michigan Medical School, oppose the granting of personhood to animals, arguing that rights holders must be able to distinguish between their own interests and what is right. "The holders of rights must have the capacity to comprehend rules of duty governing all, including themselves. In applying such rules, [they] ... must recognize possible conflicts between what is in their own interest and what is just. Only in a community of beings capable of self-restricting moral judgments can the concept of a right be correctly invoked."

Cohen rejects Singer's argument that, since a brain-damaged human could not make moral judgments, moral judgments cannot be used as the distinguishing characteristic for determining who is awarded rights. Cohen writes the test for moral judgment "is not a test to be administered to humans one by one," but should be applied to the capacity of members of the species in general.

Posner–Singer debate

Judge Richard Posner argues "facts will drive equality."

Judge Richard Posner of the United States Court of Appeals for the Seventh Circuit debated the issue of animal rights with Peter Singer on *Slate*.[104] Posner argues his moral intuition tells him "that human beings prefer their own. If a dog threatens a human infant, even if it requires causing more pain to the dog to stop it, than the dog would have caused to the infant, then we favor the child. It would be monstrous to spare the dog."

Singer challenges Posner's moral intuition by arguing formerly unequal rights for gays, women, and certain races were justified using the same set of intuitions. Posner replies equality in civil rights did not occur because of ethical arguments, but because facts mounted that there were no morally significant differences between humans based on race, sex, or sexual orientation that would support inequality. If and when similar facts emerge about the difference, or lack thereof, between humans and animals, the differences in rights will erode too. But facts will drive equality, not ethical arguments that run contrary to instinct, he argues.

Posner calls his approach "soft utilitarianism," in contrast to Singer's "hard utilitarianism." He argues: "The "soft" utilitarian position on animal rights is a moral intuition of many, probably most, Americans. We realize animals feel pain, and we think to inflict pain without a reason is bad. Nothing of practical value is added by dressing up this intuition in the language of philosophy; much is lost when the intuition is made a stage in a logical argument. When kindness toward animals is levered into a duty of weighting the pains of animals and of people equally, bizarre vistas of social engineering are opened up."

Roger Scruton

The British philosopher Roger Scruton argues that rights imply obligations. Every legal privilege, he writes, imposes a burden on the one who does not possess that privilege: that is, "your right may be my duty." Scruton therefore regards the emergence of the animal rights movement as "the strangest cultural shift within the liberal worldview," because the idea of rights and responsibilities are, he argues, distinctive to the human condition, and it makes no sense to spread them beyond our own species.

He accuses animal rights advocates of "pre-scientific" anthropomorphism, attributing traits to animals that are, he says, Beatrix Potter-like, where "only man is vile." It is within this fiction the appeal of animal rights lies, he argues. The world of animals is non-judgmental, filled with dogs who return our affection almost no matter what we do to them, and cats who pretend to be affectionate when, in fact, they care only about themselves. It is, he argues, a fantasy, a world of escape.

The shifting philosophical positions are obvious. Those positions that are presented above do not represent the greater body of the philosophical though of our culture, but that narrow slice related to animal rights and the converse thought on animal welfare. The animal rights movement has grown over the decades from the acknowledgment animals have feelings and can experience pain to the current positions of the Animal Liberation Front, PETA and the HSUS, among others. The problem exists in not everyone in the chain of documents and events understands the positions of these organizations or their origins and think of some of them as benevolent advocates for treating animals well.

The fact is, this whole evolution of philosophical thought has morphed from a concern for animals and their treatment to, in some cases, a monstrous terrorist threat both to people and animals. The challenge is to find a belief that is balanced in sound mindedness that embraces the traditional relationships with animals and their welfare, while not giving support to a planned rush to legislate the terminology, thinking and practices of the extreme animal rights agenda. It is imperative we not mix the language and thinking of those who would destroy our traditional cultural values in their attempt to dominate our world and local communities with extremist views.

That is, we are moving headlong, however unknowing that movement may be, into a vegan culture where animals are free from ownership, confinement and oversight. This will render our society pet free, breeder free and reduce our markets and restaurants to tofu only zones. Unless we stop and think of the philosophical underpinnings of where we are going, we will not like where we arrive.

Animals deserve humane treatment. I believe this. Ask my wife to tell you about my reaction to the fellow in front of Wal-Mart with a pinch collar on his Staffordshire Terrier dog. As I walked by, he wrenched on the lead, jerking the dog off of his feet. In my amazement I asked, "What in the world are you doing?" He answered tritely, "I'm teaching him to be afraid of people so he will be a good watch dog." A couple of passers-by assisted Linda in holding me back as I went for him with language inappropriate to my station in life. This was not our first incident. We attended a dog show in Central California and just watched the show, moving from ring to ring. Following one class at the Beagle ring one exhibitor, obviously angered by the judge's decision, carried his dog to his crate and threw him in with such force that he hit the back of the crate with such force that he yelped. I was on him in an instant explaining if he did not like the judge's decisions he should go hit the judge, not the dog. Again, Linda intervened and the fellow moved quickly away from me.

I do not like nor will I tolerate cruelty to animals or animal abuse. While some philosophers have contended animals do not think, reason or feel, I am quite certain they have spent no time living with a German Shepherd. But the issue is not their station in life but the need for we humans to live above that brutish level of cruelty and to recognize they, as living organisms, should be treated with respect and not subjected to unnecessary pain.

The problem with elevating animals above this level of respectful humane treatment to having 'human' rights is that the domesticated animal does not have the ability to access those rights nor to live within the privileges they convey. Rights convey a sense of responsibility, or at least they should. Rights without responsibilities provide a license for irresponsible behavior and that is evident in segments of our human world. To place those same responsibilities on our pet is to destroy them. They cannot feed themselves, provide for their own shelter, know when to defend from one person and not from the other. Their powers of discrimination are formed by their instincts, which are not always accurate in our modern world. They need to be trained and disciplined to be under control and not a menace to our communities.

This sense of human superiority and greater knowledge is the fundamental way in which animals can live with us and depend on us for direction. Without this traditional master/owner role, the animals we choose as pets would destroy themselves. They need us to be masters as much as we need them to be under control. Control does not denote a demeaning relationship but a responsible one in which the animal can relax in their role while we humans take responsibility for our decision to have them around.

If we can get our thinking straight and our beliefs in line, we can have responsible laws that protect our pets, our community and ourselves without giving human like rights to our pets who simple have no concept about or need for them.

Chapter Twenty One

The Shifting Worldview of Animals

It would be difficult to construct an accurate view of the world and of animals from the setting and mind of the first man. In fact, there would be quite a controversy in finding where to start in the concept of who and what the first humans were. If it was Adam and Eve in the garden following their creation by God, then we have the testimony of the world three major religions to consult. But if humankind is the end result of primordial slime crawling onto some prehistoric shore and evolving into modern man, we have little chance of getting into his mind.

What we do know, is the record of anthropology and archeology from artifacts and cave paintings and so forth. It is from these records we assume mankind was dependent on animals for food, clothing, weapons, instruments made of bone and other elements in their life. We also know animals were to be feared to some degree and respected in the folk lore of the hunt. Most gathering cultures had some form of ceremony around the animal who dies to give them life. In that fact of reverence and ritual is captured the bond, both physically and spiritually, between animal and human.

We are also aware of the more recent historic role of animals in the agricultural culture in which the animal was itself farmed for food, clothing and survival. But the concept of animal rights is relatively new as a part of a philosophy. How animals were treated throughout history has changed. Some of the influence for that change was religious. It is believed Hinduism goes back to about 2500 B.C., but the encoding of the belief did not happen until about 1000 B. C. Buddhism is believed to have come out of Hinduism, migrating to China in about 500 B.C. and becoming China's main religion, among others. The belief in reincarnation in each of these religious traditions and their offshoots brought with it the reverence for animals as creatures with reincarnate souls and thus worthy of respect.

Although early forms of these religions were not vegetarian, in time vegetarianism became part of the traditions as agricultural forms made that possible and practical. While this was true in some of the eastern religions, western religious tradition embraced the more ancient Jewish traditions of animal use. The Jewish tradition called for strict practices in the preparation of animals for food and which animals could be used for what purposes.

Animals have always been central to human survival and have always, until recently, been seen as useful to humanity and an essential part of human survival. The domestication of animals dates back at least as far as Adam and Eve, and the primary human attitude and view of animals probably comes out of that tradition. In Judaism and all those religions who embrace their beginnings from that tradition, God made the earth and plants, then the animals and gave them into the care and oversight of mankind. They were here for human enjoyment and use.

If one espouses Judaism, Christianity or Islam it is difficult to believe in the newer forms of animal rights and the ramifications of those beliefs, in that they are diametrically opposed to the traditional creative order of things and the purpose of creation for man in general. One could be committed to one of the newer eastern religions and hold to the animal rights agenda, although few of those traditional thought systems restrict animal from being in a close relationship with humans or being in some way used by them. Probably the closest religious thought system to our modern animal rights movement would be from the pagan belief in pantheism, the worship of nature as god.

Needless to say, today we are facing a shift in the worldview of some who are militantly committed to bring the rest of humanity into their worldview as it relates to animals. It is not however, primarily a belief that is isolated to the treatment of animals but to the worth, value and station of animals in our world. It is, for all intents and purposes a new religion. It holds that animals should not be used or enjoyed by humans in any way, shape or form. It is more than a matter of a humane treatment for our pets, it is that they should not be confined, bred, trained, eaten, used in entertainment, exhibited, or in any way held as owner for the use of humans. Animal Rights is about elevating animals to human status and being given human rights.

Here is a list of some of the animal rights objections to our traditional use of animals:

Food	Clothing	Sports & Entertainment
Bacon	Angora sweaters	Aquariums
Beef	Cashmere blazers	Bullfighting
Butter	Fur coats	Circuses
Cheese	Leather belts	Equestrian competition
Chicken	Leather jackets	Fishing
Eggs	Leather shoes	Greyhound racing
Hamburgers	Leather wallets	Horse racing
Honey	Silk scarves	Horse-drawn carriages
Kosher	Silk stockings	Hunting
slaughter	Silk ties	Magic shows using
Milk	Wool scarves &	animals
Milk chocolate	mittens	Movies with animal
Omelets	Wool sweaters	actors
Pork	Worsted wool suits	Pet ownership
Turkey		Ranching
Veal		Rodeos
		Whaling
		Zoos

The worldview of the animal rights faithful elevates animals from human personal property as found in the traditional views of God giving man responsibility for them, to being free and equal agents sharing space with humanity on earth, but being co-equal in all ways with humankind. The concept goes even further to mean if the life of an animal and the life of a human is in equal jeopardy, the value of neither is above the other. To kill the dangerous dog who is attacking the child is to do evil in choosing the life of one over the injury of the other.

"..can the slavery of animals be justified? After all, precisely what characteristic or "defect" is it that animals have that justifies our treatment of them as our slaves, as our things, as property that exists only for the sake of us, the human masters. The reality is that we progressives like to think that we have eschewed all vestiges of slavery from our lives, but the reality is that we are all slave owners, the plantation is the earth, sown with the seeds of greed, and the slaves are

134

our nonhuman sisters and brothers." Gary Francione, (Professor-Rutgers School of Law) Animal Rights Commentary, February 15, 1996

There is really no corollary in the philosophies of animal rights and animal welfare. Animal Welfare has to do with humane treatment of animals in their role with humanity. Animal Rights conversely has to do with the elevating of the status of all animals and their liberation from any relationship to humanity. They are not philosophies that exist side by side with different degrees of intensity; they are opposites - total opposites.

Given that fact, the animal rights movement has purposed to use legislative means to achieve their goals. They have not proposed we all of a sudden embrace their beliefs and practices but have designed an incremental step by step plan of cutting of the freedoms of animal owners, changing the terminology about animals relationship to the owners to 'companions,' designing animal laws as 'rights,' and moving step by step through a process of eliminating pets by anti-breeding laws ("one generation and out..."), popularizing the concept of animal rights as though it were related to animal welfare, and ultimately turning the world view of the planet into a vegan worldview.

The conclusions of this line of reason are obvious. If you eat meat, eggs, milk, cheese, or enjoy Thanksgiving dinner with your friends and family, then you cannot in good conscience cooperate with the animal rights agenda. If you wear leather products, leather shoes, belts, car seats, or other animal related products then you cannot be a supporter of the animal rights agenda. If you wear wool shirts, suits, silk or other animal fibers then you cannot support the animal rights legislative proposals. If you benefit in any way from the use of animals in farming, ranching or enjoy a rodeo, dog show or circus act or even attend

135

a zoo, then you cannot, in good conscience, go down the animal rights road without ending up with an animal rights worldview.

This is a cultural war in which a new way of looking at animals has found the fertile ground of animal legislation and the responding tender hearts of those who love them, and is incrementally moving the entire populous from a traditional cultural view of animals to a new one. That does not mean we should not have laws and the enforcement of laws to protect animals from those who abuse them and mistreat them. That does not mean we should not provide any protections from the evils that lie in the human heart. It does mean we have to become educated as to what is the underlying philosophical underpinnings of this new culture and to decide if we want to follow their lead.

If we do, count me out. I love my dogs more than you will ever know. They do not need to be equal to me for they are a part of me! We both like it that way!

Chapter Twenty Two

If You Like These Quotes...

If you like the following quotes, you will:

- Love tofu sandwiches.
- Enjoy a well made and decorated empty collar.
- Delight in an empty dog bed.
- Enjoy a well manicured back yard with no holes.
- Love the peace of no squeak toy sounds in your day.
- Get a kick out of walking through the park or on the mountain trail alone.
- Feel great about cleaning a hairless house.
- Enjoy looking through car windows without nose prints.
- Enjoy opening the mail to find no bills or reminders from your veterinarian.
- Enjoy weekends free from travel to dog shows.
- Delight in going out to dinner at your favorite ~~steak~~ tofu house.
- Love the taste of fresh water on your cereal in the morning.
- ... - and so on...

Wayne Pacelle: (President of the Humane Society of the United States, former Executive Director of Fund for Animals). Pacelle grew up in New Haven, CT, and began his animal rights activist career by setting up the Student Animal Rights Coalition at Yale University. In 1988 he became executive director of Fund for Animals, joining HSUS in 1994.

"One generation and out. We have no problems with the extinction of domestic animals. They are creations of human selective breeding."

"Like any kind of sophisticated political operation, you use the best research tools in order to drive your message, but in terms of our policy formulations, I can't think of a time that we've done research."

"We believe in the Three Rs - reducing the consumption of meat and other animal-based foods; refining the diet by eating products only from methods of production, transport, and slaughter that minimize pain and distress; and replacing meat and other animal-based foods in the diet with plant-based foods." (Posted in a blog, Mar. 30, 2009, and reproduced in "The three R's of the HSUS agenda," by Susan Crowell, *Farm & Dairy Magazine*, Apr. 2, 2009)

"I want to achieve greater effectiveness and create an even more powerful organization to advance major social changes. ... I've tried to focus the organization on a few key reforms because I believe the only way we are going to achieve change is by putting enough muscle behind specific campaigns - to change the views of policy-makers, corporate decision-makers, and get issues into the media - and to create a grassroots movement to drive these issues forward. So we're first focusing on factory farming, the greatest of all animal abuses as measured in terms of animals involved and the duration and acuteness of their suffering."
(In an interview with *Satya* magazine, June 2005)

"Do we want to see an end to the fur industry? I think HSUS offers the best potential to get us there..."
(In an interview with *Satya* magazine, June 2005)

"The entire animal rights movement in the United States reacted with unfettered glee at the ban in England ... We view this act of parliament as one of the most important actions in the history of the animal rights movement. This will energize our

138

efforts to stop hunting with hounds." (Quoted in *The Times* [London], Dec. 26, 2004)

"Public opinion surveys demonstrate time and time again that Americans care about the humane treatment of animals and that sentiment is being translated into policy with several major animal protection provisions in the farm bill." (Quoted in "More Than Subsidies in Farm Bill," by James Henry, for AgriNews Publications, Illinois, Apr. 25, 2002)

"We have no ethical obligation to preserve the different breeds of livestock produced through selective breeding. ... One generation and out. We have no problem with the extinction of domestic animals. They are creations of human selective breeding."
(Quoted in *Animal People*, May, 1993)

"The definition of obscenity on the newsstands should be extended to many hunting magazines."
(Quoted in *Bloodties: Nature, Culture and the Hunt*, by Ted Kerasote, p. 266, 1993)

'When asked if he envisioned a future without pets, "If I had my personal view, perhaps that might take hold. In fact, I don't want to see another dog or cat born'."
(Quoted in *Bloodties: Nature, Culture and the Hunt*, by Ted Kerasote, p. 266, 1993)

"If we could shut down all sport hunting in a moment, we would."
(Quoted in "Impassioned Agitator," Associated Press, Dec. 30, 1991. Doubtless among other publications, this AP article ran in the Kingman Daily Miner (AZ) on the same date. Yet in a June 30, 2009 interview with AgriTalk, Pacelle denied that he ever said this.)

139

"Our goal is to get sport hunting in the same category as cock fighting and dog fighting. Our opponents say that hunting is a tradition. We say traditions can change."

(Quoted in *Bozeman Daily Chronicle*, Oct. 8, 1991)

"Only 7% of Americans are hunters. That means there are more of us than there are of them. It is simply a matter of democracy. The majority rules in a democracy. We are going to use the ballot box and the democratic process to stop all hunting in the United States. ... We will take it species by species until all hunting is stopped in California. Then we will take it state by state."

(Interviewed for *Full Cry Magazine*, "America's leading tree hound publication," Oct. 1, 1990

Ingrid Newkirk: National Director of PETA (People for the Ethical Treatment of Animals)

"Pet ownership is an absolutely abysmal situation brought about by human manipulation."

"For one thing we would no longer allow breeding. People could not create different breeds. If people had companion animals in their homes, these animals would have to be refugees from the animal shelter and the streets … But as the surplus of cats and dogs declined, eventually companion animals would be phased out and we would return to a more symbiotic relationship - enjoyment at a distance."

"One Day, we would like an end to pet shops and the breeding of animals. (Dogs) would pursue their natural lives in the wild... They would have full lives, not waiting at home for someone to come home in the evenings and pet them and then sit there and watch TV." - *(Where Would We Be Without Animals?" Chicago Daily Herald Mar. 1, 1990)*

"Animal liberations do not separate out the human animal, so there is no rational basis for saying that a human being has special rights. A rat is a pig is a dog is a boy. They're all mammals." -*(Vogue, September, 1989)*

"Humans have grown like a cancer. We're the biggest blight on the face of the earth." -*(Reader's Digest June, 1990)*

"Even if animal tests produced a cure [for AIDS], 'we'd be against it.'" as quoted in Fred Barnes, "Politics," Vogue, September 1989, p. 542.

"If my father had a heart attack, it would give me no solace at all to know his treatment was first tried on a dog," Ingrid Newkirk, national director for People for the Ethical Treatment of Animals, (PETA), Washington Post, Nov. 13, 1983.

Michael Fox, Head of HSUS's Center for Respect for Life and Environment:

"The life of an ant and the life of my child should be granted equal consideration."

(Expressing opposition to use of bug sprays) "Only a few of the million you kill would have bitten you." (In *Returning to Eden*, Fox publication)

"Anthropocentrism, regarding human kind as the very center and pinnacle of existence, is a disease of arrested development." (Speech "A Vision Shared: What We Are Fighting For," to the World Congress for Animals, Washington, D.C., June 20, 1996)

"We are not superior. There are no clear distinctions between us   and   animals." (*Washingtonian Magazine*, February 1990)

"The life of an ant and that of my child should be granted equal   consideration."
(In *Inhumane Society*, 1990)

"The life of an ant and the life of my child should be accorded equal respect."
(Associated Press, Jan. 15, 1989)

"Human care (of animals) is simply sentimental, sympathetic patronage."
(*Newsweek* interview, 1988)

"Man is the most dangerous, destructive, selfish and unethical animal on earth."
(Quoted in The Intellectual Activist, Sept. 14, 1983)

(Inhumane Society, Fox Publications) "Humane treatment is just sentimental, sympathetic patronage."

"Dr. Michael Fox of the Humane Society says that 'pet owner' is offensive too and should be changed to 'human companion of the nonhuman companion'" - *(S. News and World Report 1992)*

Kim Bartlett, Merritt Clifton, Editors of the Animal Activist Publication Animal People:

"Statistics generally don't support the claim that purebred enthusiasts are responsible for more than a fraction of the pet overpopulation problem, but anti-breeding ordinances tend to target (breeders) because (they) can be identified and regulated much more easily than people who simply let unaltered animals roam." - *(Animal People, May, 1993)*

Tom Regan, Q & A session following speech, "Animal Rights, Human Wrongs," University of Wisconsin-Madison, October   27,   1989:
(Answering a question whether he would save a dog or a baby if a boat capsized in the ocean.)

142

"If it were a retarded baby and bright dog, I'd save the dog."

Gary Francione, Director of the Rutgers Animal Rights Law Clinic; and Tom Regan, Philosophy Professor, North Carolina State University:

"Not only are the philosophies of animal rights and animal welfare separated by irreconcilable differences ... *the enactment of animal welfare measures actually impedes the achievement of animal rights*" (emphasis added). "A Movement's Means Create Its Ends," *Animal Agenda* January-February, 1992, pp. 40-42.

The Animal Voice Vol. 4, No. 2, pp. 54-56: "The theory of animal rights is not consistent with the theory of animal welfare ... Animal rights means dramatic social changes for humans and nonhumans alike; if our bourgeois values prevent us from accepting those changes, then we have no right to call ourselves advocates of human rights."

Bruce Friedrich, PETA Spokesperson at the "Animal Rights 2001" convention

"It would be great if all the fast-food outlets, slaughterhouses, these laboratories and the banks who fund them exploded tomorrow... Hallelujah to the people who are willing to do it."

Peter Singer, Animal Liberation: A New Ethic for Our Treatment of Animals, 2nd ed. (New York Review of Books, 1990),Preface, p. ii.

"We are not especially 'interested in' animals. Neither of us had ever been inordinately fond of dogs, cats, or horses in the way that many people are. We didn't 'love' animals." --

Alex Pacheco, Director, PETA

"Arson, property destruction, burglary and theft are 'acceptable crimes' when used for the animal cause." Barbara Biel, The Animals' Agenda, Vol 15 #3.

"...the animal rights movement is not concerned about species extinction. An elephant is no more or less important than a cow, just as a dolphin is no more important than a tuna...(In fact, many animal rights advocates would argue that it is better for the chimpanzee to become extinct than to be exploited continually in laboratories, zoos and circuses."

Bill Maher, PETA celebrity spokesman

"To those people who say, `My father is alive because of animal experimentation,' I say `Yeah, well, good for you. This dog died so your father could live.' Sorry, but I am just not behind that kind of trade off."

Chris DeRose, director, Last Chance for Animals, as quoted in Elizabeth Venant and David Treadwell, "Biting Back," Los Angeles Times, April 12, 1990, p. E12.

"If the death of one rat cured all diseases, it wouldn't make any difference to me."

Tom Regan, as quoted in David T. Hardy, "America's New Extremists: What You Need to Know About the Animal Rights Movement." (Washington, DC: Washington Legal Foundation, 1990), p. 8.

"If it [abolition of animal research] means there are some things we cannot learn, then so be it. We have no basic right not to be harmed by those natural diseases we are heir to."

"Even granting that we [humans] face greater harm than laboratory animals presently endure if ... research on these animals is stopped, the animal rights view will not be satisfied with anything less than total abolition." (Tom Regan, The Case for Animal Rights, 1983).

Mary Beth Sweetland, PETA

"I'm an insulin-dependent diabetic. Twice a day I take synthetically manufactured insulin that still contains some animal products--and I have no qualms about it." Sweetland adds, "I don't see myself as a hypocrite. I need my life to fight for the rights of animals."

"Liberating our language by eliminating the word 'pet' is the first step...In an ideal society where all exploitation and oppression has been eliminated, it will be NJARA's policy to oppose the keeping of animals as 'pets.'" --New Jersey Animal Rights Alliance, "Should Dogs Be Kept As Pets? NO!" Good Dog! February 1991, p. 20.

John Bryant, Fettered Kingdoms: An Examination of A Changing Ethic (Washington, DC: People for the Ethical Treatment of Animals (PETA), 1982), p. 15.

"Let us allow the dog to disappear from our brick and concrete jungles--from our firesides, from the leather nooses and chains by which we enslave it." --

Goodwin, J.P.

The following quotes were made during Goodwin's time with the Coalition to Abolish the Fur Trade. However, he was working for Wayne Pacelle of the HSUS as early as 1997. (Blunt CEO defends Humane Society from attack dogs, *Press-Telegram*, (Long Beach, CA), Aug. 25, 2007.) Goodwin has described himself as an "ALF graduate" (Anti-fur groups wage war on mink farms, *New York Times*, Sept. 2, 1996), and as a "former member" of the Animal Liberation Front ("Guerrillas say they fight to help liberate animals; FBI considers group's members domestic terrorists", *Dallas Morning News*, Feb. 15, 1998). See also Careers in the conflict industry: HSUS and the making of a conflict industrialist, FCUSA commentary, Aug. 21, 2001.

"We have found that civil disobedience and direct action has been powerful in generating massive attention in our

145

communities ... and has been very effective in traumatizing our targets." (National Animal Rights Convention '97, June 27, 1997)

"We're ecstatic," said Goodwin, who believes all living things are equal. "We have no problem with inanimate objects being destroyed so animate objects can survive. We believe life is more valuable than property."

(Quoted in "Activists take credit for Sandy fur fire," by Cala Byram, *The Deseret News*, Mar. 11, 1997, on learning of a bomb attack that destroyed the Utah Fur Breeders Agricultural Cooperative. A caretaker and his family were asleep in the building at the time.)

"We've started picketing outside the homes of the [department store] executives because these minks on these fur farms never get a chance to go home and relax. Those executives do not deserve a break. They do not deserve to go home and rest."
(Speech "No More Fur: Bringing the Fur Industry To Its Knees," World Congress for Animals, Washington, D.C., June 20, 1996)

"It's time for the animal rights movement to take this industry and drive the final nail into the coffin by whatever means it takes. If that means being outside the executives houses, if that means blockading their doors, whatever it takes."
(Speech "No More Fur: Bringing the Fur Industry To Its Knees," World Congress for Animals, Washington, D.C., June 20, 1996)

"Let it be stated loud and clear, that myself and the Coalition to Abolish the Fur Trade support these actions 100%. We will never, ever, ever work with anyone who helps the FBI stop the A.L.F.."
(In Fur wars heat up: A.L.F. is on the warpath!" by J.P.

146

Goodwin, on ALF attacks against fur farms, *No Compromise*, issue 4, 1996)

"My goal is the abolition of all animal agriculture." (As quoted on AR-Views, an animal rights Internet discussion group)

"If the feed barn, and processing barns are away from the animals, and downwind, then they could be burned down. Otherwise mink releases are the only way to go." (As quoted on AR-Views, an animal rights Internet discussion group)

See also: HSUS and the Making of a Conflict Industrialist FCUSA commentary on the career of J.P. Goodwin, Aug. 12, 2001.

Chapter Twenty Three

A Manifesto

There is a natural alliance between the rancher and the farmer, who raise animals for human use and consumption, and those who have pets and love their animals – some of whom pursue animal sports. That affinity is becoming something of a necessity as the animal rights movement paints us all with one brush stroke and positions itself against the human/animal connection.

We are not joined in a massive organization like many who oppose us, yet we must come to understand where we stand and why if we are to survive the onslaught of Animal Rights groups and their relentless push to legislate us out of existence.

With that in mind I propose the following as a manifesto for the animal welfare people, like myself, who love animals, use agricultural animal products and are not about to be pushed into an animal-free world by this new culture of legalism.

1. We believe in the right of the people – any people – to own animals as pets and to enjoy activities with their animal friends.

2. We believe the fundamental right to life, liberty and the pursuit of happiness includes the historic relationship between people and their animals, and this right should not be infringed upon.

3. We believe that animals have limited abilities to understand and access the legal structures of human law and courts and that they should not be accorded rights

appropriate for humans, but are the private property of their owners.

4. We believe all animals should be accorded humane treatment and not be abused.

5. We believe political jurisdictions should pass laws and enforce them to protect animals from abuse and provide for animal welfare.

6. We believe political jurisdictions should limit themselves to matters of animal welfare and not step into the arena of animal rights, dictating to the owners of animals whether or not an animal should be spayed, neutered, bred or used in the natural process of reproduction.

7. We believe political jurisdictions should not reward the irresponsible pet owner by rescuing their mistakes while punishing the responsible pet owner with breeding limitations.

8. While negotiating these differences in oversight of animal care may be difficult, we believe that political jurisdictions are charged with that task nonetheless, and should refrain from blanket legislation that punishes the responsible and violates their right to enjoy their animals and to reproduce suitable animals for future generations.

9. We believe some animals are useful to humanity as food, clothing and other lawful things, and legislation to protect those animals from cruelty should be framed by and with consultation by those involved in animal agriculture and not by those who oppose the human use of animals.

10. We believe breed specific legislation is a breach of freedom by those legislative bodies who propose them, and that animal behavior and owner behavior are issues for legislation (not the color of the species or its body shape or

any arbitrary category by which an animal is legislated out of existence simply because of its assumed breed.)

11. We believe those who object to the eating of animal products should not eat animal products, as they choose without legislation to prohibit others from doing so.

12. We believe those who do not object to eating and using animal products should not be prohibited from doing so by those who do.

13. We believe the essence of human freedom rests on the honoring of individual choices and resulting responsibilities and the law should deal with bad behavior and not with the nature of individual choice.

14. We do not believe the animal rights agenda is beneficial to human freedom, nor is it a course of action to follow in creating a better world.

15. We do not believe animals will be better off by following the animal rights agenda, for they need the oversight of responsible owners.

16. We do not believe changing the wording of legislative definition to make those people having oversight of animals from "owner" to "guardian" is a good thing for the animals and complicates the relationship of responsible people to their animals.

17. We believe animal owners are best qualified to speak for their animals and animal rights organizations who do not have 'care responsibility' for the animal should not be considered spokespersons for owned animals.

18. We believe there is danger in the sweeping extremes being considered in today's legislative euphoria. We therefore urge caution on the part of government officials and legislators.

19. We believe the incremental tightening of laws on the general public who are responsible citizens and law-abiding, is in danger of crushing the freedoms this nation was founded upon. We therefore urge legislatures to consider how to 'not' legislate rather than support an endless string of ever increasing laws and regulations.

20. We do not believe domesticated animals should be released into the wild to face the dangers of nature. We propose that Mother Nature is a cruel taskmaster who deals harshly with her subjects and is often a serial killer.

Chapter Twenty Four

A Battle Plan

Carl von Clausewitz is credited with the saying, "The first rule of warfare is to gain public opinion." When asked how to gain public opinion, he reportedly responded, "Win battles."

One of the enigmas of modern conflict is the phenomenon of the current War on Terror. The loosely organized enemies of America were not a nation but a philosophy. Warfare had traditionally been conducted by cultural interests that inhabit a territory, defined by boundaries. Nations do war with nations. But in this case a philosophy declared war on the United States 20 years before we accepted the challenge and rose to the occasion. We simply did not know how to respond to a non-traditional cultural element that could not be territorially or nationally defined. The war was between a non-nation and a nation. This has frustrated traditional thinking ever since.

During this period of a declared war that we were ignoring, over 20 incidents of violent attacks occurred against our interests without incurring any response. U. S. inaction caused rising public opinion within the camps of the enemy and rejoicing at their victories. The culture that gave context to this philosophy, although not participating in the acts of war totally, had come to admire and rejoice in the victories of their fellows. The terrorist organizations had gained public opinion.

Our response was militarily sound, in a traditional sense, but it did not garner popular public opinion that we needed to sustain the effort. Then came General David Petraeus, whose battle plan added elements of society-building into the military operation. The soldiers were dispersed into the culture and performed a dual role. One was to respond militarily as would be expected in war, but the other was a new twist on Von Clausewitz. The soldiers were assigned areas of the community to rebuild and to befriend. They built schools, roads, fire stations; they guarded community activities and in general lived as part of the foreign community they inhabited. The end result was they became less of an occupation force and more of a liberating force. They gained public opinion.

In the war on pets and agricultural animals, we are facing large well-funded organizations that have gained public opinion. They have platformed themselves as the champion of the animals – speaking for them, standing foursquare against abuse – and style themselves as caretakers of abused animals. They sold the American people an illusion without content. They, in fact, do not care for animals; they only propose legislation to eliminate animals from human control. They do not take care of the abused; they only take pictures for more public relations commercials. Their persona does not match their performance. Yet, it has worked to garner public opinion and to reap the rewards of multiplied millions of dollars into their coffers.

How then do we approach the task of defeating their attack on real animal lovers and caretakers of our land? How do we gain public opinion? How do we overcome the onslaught of well-financed, paid lobbyists working full-time in every state to accomplish the illusionary goals of these Animal Rights advocates? I believe there are many fronts that need to be addressed if we are to ever stop this culture shift that threatens to ultimately leave us without pets or agricultural animals.

1. Coordinate without organizing.

It may sound like a dichotomous statement but let me explain. If you've ever seen a re-enactment of an old battle it is almost humorous by modern standards. The Continental armies would march to face each other, then line up in ranks and shoot at each other until there was no one left standing on one side. It was not until the American Revolution that battle tactics changed. It was the American Indian who taught us to fight. They did not stand in rows facing the enemy, but hid and fought by subterfuge. The rules of honor were thrown away, in fact, in war, there were no rules. In this setting guerilla warfare was discovered and readily adapted. The American troops then did not "play fair" with the British, ambushing at will.

One of the illusions of warfare is it needs to be fair and honorable. The assumption is that our well-organized opponent must be faced with a well-organized counter force. But it is possible for a well-coordinated grass roots force from various sectors, various sports and various affected groups to defeat the corporate structures of the Animal Rights movement. In fact, we may find it far more effective to be 'guerrillas' so to speak, fighting in many ways on many fronts without trying to gather all elements into one super organization. To attempt to do so would expend a tremendous amount of energy gaining agreement, gathering leadership and determining tactics. But, it is possible independent guerrilla cells can effect greater change by being within a coordinated communications network where all effected organizations and groups work from their 'hiding place' so to speak, attacking at will with whatever issues they feel passionate about.

Right now there are hundreds of rising cells, groups, organizations, communications networks, clubs and interests, connecting on the internet, by mailing lists, email lists and other means. If each continues and intensifies its efforts, it may well be that our sworn enemy will not be able to identify their opposition and will be hampered in their counter attack. This is the principle of guerrilla action where the objective is the same, but the cells operate independently. Because it does not require a high degree of cooperation or agreement, it avoids one of the problems with gathering independent groups together; that is the issues arising from within. Without that requirement of agreement, each can be free to move forward without permission from the others. Another problem to avoid is where one person or group becomes so radical as to act in a way that discredits the entire group. That is why a simple and straightforward manifesto will be important – creating a movement that is coordinated, one that does not just stir emotions and randomly participate in confusion.

If we can commit to similar principles, communicate freely within the various structures already present, then we can be interdependent without competing with our sworn enemy for buildings, organizational structures and leadership. We can come at them from all sides, and with reasoned logic expose their hidden agenda.

2. Expose the real agenda.

It is hard to view the sad brown eyes of the puppy with tears running down the side of its face and say, "No, I will not help you!" The presumption is set up; and the music, lighting and story all convey one unmistakable message: This is an abused puppy that will die unless someone gives just $19.00 a month. The fact is, it may be a borrowed pet. And other than the deceptive makeup, it is well-cared-for and happy. This is another

155

Animal Rights commercial asking people to presumably save the life of the unfortunate puppy, whose life was never in jeopardy anyway.

Such are the illusions of Hollywood movie-making, where cut-and-paste sound bites and visual icons, are all put together to capture the emotional effect desired by the producer. We laugh, we cry, we get excited and we become ill all because of the skill of the producer in putting together the entertainment or commercials we view. Politics has skillfully used visual and audio effects to present their candidate in a happy, competent pose while showing their competition with their mouth opened, nose wrinkled and an angry scowl. It is not reality, it is a production. It is designed to accomplish a purpose, and production can tell any story regardless of the truth. Truth is not reality, perception is reality.

So we have to concentrate on getting the truth packaged and presented in a way that both exposes the hidden agenda and also present the truth in a way that captures the heart of the nation. We have to expose the truth – make it the perception as well as the reality.

3. Create Public Opinion

One of the tactics of conflict is to demonize your opposition. The animal rights movement has the jump on us. It has incrementally demonized the animal world, where humans are involved with animals. Breeders are evil for they cause the overpopulation of pets that have to be euthanized. Hunters are evil because they shoot unsuspecting animals grazing in pristine meadows. Farmers are evil because they mistreat their animals and feed them steroids. Ranchers are evil because, well, just because. And on goes the list with the attached imagery of terror

156

being rained upon defenseless animals who are held against their will by their captors.

The reality is quite the reverse. Those who live with animals and raise them and depend on them have a higher level of respect for them than the anti-animal people have or will ever understand. The problem is, the other side has spent millions of dollars characterizing the evils of animal ownership, while we who actually live with and love animals have not spent a dime defending ourselves/ putting a positive image out there. The general public and the legislators who are targeted with this stuff do not know any better. They actually believe the well-presented lies.

This phenomenon will not change until we change it. Animal food manufacturers, ranchers, farmers, the poultry industry, pet stores, pet publishers, dog clubs, and every pet owner and business owner who has any tie to animals as pets or as an agricultural product must get involved in creating public opinion. Unless we do, we are one animal generation away from being without pets and out of business.

Again, this does not argue that animal abuse does not occur, not does it argue for any justification for it. Legislation against animal cruelty and abuse is justified and to be encouraged. But as evil as murder is, we cannot stop it by eliminating people. Similarly, the elimination of animals as pets is not a legitimate way to stop animal abuse.

4. Educate Children

The Animal Rights movement has already targeted schools and have produced texts and study materials to sell their agenda. As we move forward we must educate the school systems about the difference between animal rights and animal welfare and provide sound and balanced materials which address animal welfare. This can be a gigantic effort, yet it needs to be encouraged by everyone who is legitimately involved with animals.

5. Educate Legislators

I was rather shocked when a Lieutenant from a local police department, teaching at my academy class, defined a jury as "ignorance multiplied by 12." Then as he continued to talk, I understood what he was saying and had to agree. Jurors are selected from the common profile of the community by random drawing, and they are ignorant. That is, they do not know everything, and usually they are not lawyers or police officers so they know little of the finer elements of the law. They are not stupid, but they are without a graduate education on the issues they will be hearing/ deciding in court. They are ignorant, and our system of justice had been designed to use that naiveté as a place to form a seemingly reasonable opinion as to what ought to be.

Similarly, legislators are elected because of their stance on broad issues, though they are seldom knowledgeable about the difference between animal welfare and animal rights. They have to be educated so they understand. The problem is, again, the animal rights people are way ahead of us, having assigned paid lobbyists in almost every state to sell their imagery, their agenda and their expertise. From that platform they present their legislation, and before we even know what is happening we are legislated out of existence.

We simply have to catch up. We must make folks aware of the issues that are being presented and even come to the place we are sponsoring legislation that protects us from the sort of catch

22 we find ourselves in. We have to go to the legislative session, find the right committees and reverse this incremental trend, or we will be legislated out of existence.

6. Communicate

Every part of the animal industry and business world (as well as the pet club and organization) has to begin to communicate, not just our presence and our products, but to share our stance on the value of our animals to us and to mankind. While the animal rights agenda has communicated the value of an animal-free world, we need to do the exact opposite, and do it better and more frequently than they do.

It has been said that the most-believed item is oft repeated misinformation. That is where we are today with this issue. Whatever it takes, we have to reverse that trend and replace the misinformation with truth. The truth will set us free.

7. Give

There are costs involved in educating, publishing and lobbying. The Animal Rights people have done a great job of raising money, even if their methods are less than honorable. To compete, every business that involves animals has to set aside a budget item to protect their future. This must include legal expenses and marketing costs. Each organization that enters the arena of battle needs to unabashedly raise money but be careful not to handle it as our opponents have. The Animal Rights movements have brought discredit upon themselves by their financial excesses and the less than straightforward manner in which the funds they have raised have been handled and spent. We have to do better. Possibly we need an umbrella organization who will do an annual audit of organizations and businesses involved, and honor them with an approval status. We cannot allow ourselves to bring dishonor to our effort.

8. Become Political

'Politics' has become a dirty word, not because it should be, but because of the craziness that happens in the political world. The fact is, politics is simply the way in which groups of people manage and conduct their affairs. All groups have political issues, structures and rules. Some of those rules are unspoken, but they are real, nonetheless.

Most animal people are much like myself. I've been around people all my life in various people centered jobs and activities and I prefer my dogs. Animal people, whether pet owners or farmers, ranchers or animal sports people, are usually rough and rugged, honest people who prefer to be alone or with their animals. They are the kinds of neighbors you would be lucky to have. They will help you out when you need it but will leave you alone to be yourself if you don't. But we cannot win this war alone in the mountains. We simply have to come together - form up.

Each community needs to gather around its various animal-related businesses and become involved in the political process at the grass roots level. There are some candidates for political office that may need our endorsement and there are certainly some who need to be booted out of office in the next election. We need to interview them, talk to them and even run for office. This needs to become a political issue for each of us.

9. Challenge the Law

While law-abiding citizens, we need not support and submit to illegitimate laws; it is unconstitutional. There are laws so convoluted and ill-conceived they are blatantly unconstitutional. Resistance to unjust law is part of our heritage.

Our first and foremost document as a nation, the Declaration of Independence, addressed the issue of unjust governance with these words:

> *We hold these truths to be self-evident, that all men are created equal, that they are endowed by their Creator with certain unalienable Rights, that among these are Life, Liberty and the pursuit of Happiness. — That to secure these rights, Governments are instituted among Men, deriving their just powers from the consent of the governed, — That whenever any Form of Government becomes destructive of these ends, it is the Right of the People to alter or to abolish it, and to institute new Government, laying its foundation on such principles and organizing its powers in such form, as to them shall seem most likely to effect their Safety and Happiness. Prudence, indeed, will dictate that Governments long established should not be changed for light and transient causes; and accordingly all experience hath shewn that mankind are more disposed to suffer, while evils are sufferable than to right themselves by abolishing the forms to which they are accustomed. But when a long train of abuses and usurpations, pursuing invariably the same Object evinces a design to reduce them under absolute Despotism, it is their right, it is their duty, to throw off such Government, and to provide new Guards for their future security. — Such has been the patient sufferance of these Colonies; and such is now the necessity which constrains them to alter their former Systems of Government.*

It is not just our right, but our duty to restrain government from restricting our freedom to life – a quiet and peaceful life in the fear of God. There is some really terrible legislation being passed these days that must be resisted by our vote, by the courts and by peaceful noncompliance if necessary.

10. Add your own item

This is certainly not a complete list of items or of issues. We have been invited to a war. Rather, war has been declared upon us and unless we respond, we will lose. It is my hope that sound minded and gentle souls will hear these words and stand strong against the onslaught we are facing. For hundreds of years our American heritage and our culture has lived in peace with our animals. We have enjoyed the best of things, but now come to the time when a novel culture without animals has risen and decided we should not exist. They insist that all adopt their values and way of life, move from the country, enter the confusion of the city, and eat tofu. For me, the path is clear: Give me my animals and my way of life or just shoot me. My diet is between me and my doctor, and my enjoyment of my dogs is not optional.

Resources

The Declaration of Independence
James Sperell PhD -
www.apdt.com/conf/archive/2006/speakers/bio_serpell.aspx
http://www.birdcompanions.com/Flyer%20-%20AW_VS_AR.pdfJune 2005 interview, *Satya* magazine.
http://satyamag.com/
http://homepages.sover.net/~lsudlow/ARvsAW.htm
http://pipl.com/directory/people/Miyun/Park
http://www.pet-law.com/index.php?option=com_content&view=article&id=32&Itemid=13
http://www.consumerfreedom.com/?gclid=CKz315rRt6UCFQYHbAodRAsNaQ
http://www.crbeagles.com/misc/HSUS.htm
http://www.americananimalwelfare.com/rights.html
http://www.furcommission.com/debate/
http://www.animalscam.com/rights_vs_welfare.cfm
http://www.animalscam.com/rights_vs_welfare.cfm
http://www.thedogpress.com/SideEffects/AR-Defined-09023.asp
http://www.exposeanimalrights.com/animal_rights.html
http://www.naiaonline.org/articles/archives/animalright.htm

http://www.nwcoa.com/pr/index.htm
http://www.ncraoa.com/AR_VS_AW.html
http://www.toybreeds.com/animal_welfare_vs_animal_rights.ht
m
http://petbreedersandowners.com/
http://www.naiaonline.org/articles/archives/bldties.htm
http://purebredcatbreedrescue.org/animal_rights.htm
http://www.consumerfreedom.com/news_detail.cfm/h/2054-the-
inhumane-society-of-the-united-states